Decision Criteria for New Product Acceptance and Success

Decision Criteria for New Product Acceptance and Success

THE ROLE OF TRADE BUYERS

EDWARD W. McLAUGHLIN
AND **VITHALA R. RAO**

QUORUM BOOKS
New York • Westport, Connecticut • London

Library of Congress Cataloging-in-Publication Data

McLaughlin, Edward W. (Edward William)
  Decision criteria for new product acceptance and success : the
role of trade buyers / Edward W. McLaughlin and Vithala R. Rao.
    p. cm.
  Includes bibliographical references and index.
  ISBN 0-89930-525-3 (alk. paper)
  1. Grocery trade – United States.   2. New products – United States –
Management. I. Rao, Vithala R. II. Title.
HD9321.5.M28 1991
664'.068'5 – dc20   90-26408

British Library Cataloguing in Publication Data is available.

Library of Congress Catalog Card Number: 90-26408
ISBN: 0-89930-525-3

First published in 1991

Quorum Books, One Madison Avenue, New York, NY 10010
An imprint of Greenwood Publishing Group, Inc.

Printed in the United States of America

The paper used in this book complies with the
Permanent Paper Standard issued by the National
Information Standards Organization (Z39.48–1984).

10 9 8 7 6 5 4 3 2 1

CONTENTS

ILLUSTRATIONS

FIGURES

TABLES

EXHIBITS

PREFACE

Despite the rapid surge of new product introductions into the grocery product distribution system (over 12,000 in 1989), relatively little is known regarding the process and acceptance criteria of trade buyers, yet the role trade buyers play is critical for the marketplace success of new products.

This book examines the processes followed in developing and introducing new products, by both manufacturers and trade intermediaries. First, the overall structure of the U.S. grocery distribution is described. The various strategies of manufacturers and retailers are very much determined by the organizational setting in which new product introductions take place. Next, the key participants in the new product introduction process are discussed, and their standard operating procedures are outlined.

This background is vital to an understanding of the balance of the book. We present a broad framework for analyzing new product introductions and explain methodologies useful in this process. We then describe the extensive research we have conducted on new product acceptance by trade buyers drawing on three sources of data—publicly available information on new products, survey data collected on actual buyer decisions on over 2,000 new products, and buyer decisions on hypothetical descriptions of new products—and put forth the statistical results on the relative importance of the criteria employed by supermarket buyers in their decisions to accept (or reject) a new product offered to them. Based on these results, several management tools, including an expert system, are developed. Finally, the implications of these results for marketing managers, procurement executives, and public policy makers are discussed.

This book integrates much scholarly research and industry information never before assembled in one place. It is designed as a reference book for practitioners involved in the many stages of new product development, as well as for students of the process. We hope that the book will shed light on the many and complex ways that the new product introduction process works and how managers might benefit from this knowledge. It is our intention that this book will serve as a stimulus for conducting the continued empirical research needed for the improved efficiency performance of the new product introduction process.

We are grateful for the help of numerous individuals in the preparation of this book. We are indebted to the team of supermarket buyers, who prefer to remain anonymous, for allowing us to collect the data necessary for the research and for the endless questions and meetings that they patiently endured. We thank Rod Hawkes, Sudeep Haldar, and David Russo for their assistance in several phases of this research and Barb Guile for her expert typing of early drafts of this manuscript.

Decision Criteria for New Product Acceptance and Success

1

NEW PRODUCTS IN THE U.S. DISTRIBUTION SYSTEM

Distribution of goods and services in the United States includes a vast array of networks, products, functions, and economic agents or players. The set of these phenomena that are brought together to support and develop the distribution system for any particular product is a direct consequence of the nature of the product and the institutions that surround it. These relationships are generally quite complex. They vary as a function of product volume, ownership patterns, financial arrangements, cultural constraints, and, of course, the specific elements of the firm's marketing strategy. This last dimension encompasses a considerable number of critical decisions regarding the product's target customer, positioning, pricing, and promotional and advertising strategy.

Distribution systems (a term used throughout this book roughly interchangeably with the term *marketing channels*) take years to build, include large numbers of independent companies, and are not changed easily. Louis W. Stern and Adel I. El-Ansey describe marketing channels as "sets of interdependent organizations involved in the process of making a product or service available for use or consumption" (Kotler, 1988, p. 553). In essence, complex marketing channels exist because the myriad of factors, functions, and intermediaries that must be addressed in order to ensure the delivery of a product or service to its ultimate end user cannot possibly all be controlled by the producer alone in most instances.

Initial producers of raw materials depend on other organizations to overcome the critical differences in form, time, place, and possession that typically distinguish products in their raw commodity state from the state desired for final use by consumers. To accomplish these tasks, marketing intermediary organizations engage in a wide spectrum of activities, generally encompassing financing, ownership transfer, transportation and storage, risk taking, communication (e.g., order taking), negotiation, advertising and promotion, and market research. In many industries the range of distribution activities is so broad that their total worth, or value added, exceeds considerably the producer value of the original product. In the U.S. food system, for example, farmers receive less than one-third of consumer expenditures for food in retail stores. The remaining approximately two-thirds is required to cover the further processing and distribution activities (Gallo, 1990). In 1989, $134 billion was paid to suppliers for their raw agricultural and fishery products; the downstream food system firms added about $495 billion in additional value in the forms of transportation, storing, further processing and so forth. Hence, at least for 1989, food processors, transporters, and retail-type firms contributed nearly 80 percent of the total value of food.

Regardless of the particular distribution system or strategy, buying and selling of new products, and, in particular, their initial introduction into their respective distribution systems, constitutes a critically important component in determining the overall success of any business entity. Indeed, new products often are the means by which change and progress are introduced into an industry, thereby improving overall industry performance and consumer satisfaction.

U.S. GROCERY DISTRIBUTION SYSTEMS

It may be safely argued that in no industry are new products more important than in the grocery segment of the industry classification broadly referred to as consumer products. The number of new products in this segment is far larger than any other group of industries, due primarily to a general lack of technical complexity, the fact that the products are easily described, and they often constitute a significant proportion of the overall sales of their respective companies. Moreover, data on new products in the grocery distribution system are available, in some cases, even with historical comparisons. It is also true that the research and development techniques, sales approaches, and buyer-seller market structures in the grocery distribution system are fairly representative of a much broader group of industries and distribution systems. Grocery products includes food and nonfood items. For all these reasons, the majority of the processes described and the work reported in this book refer to this one vast distribution system: the U.S. grocery products system.

Figure 1.1 describes the major marketing channels in the U.S. grocery distribution system. The few channels not indicated on this figure (e.g., farmer markets and roadside stands) may be considered insignificant in terms of their total system value contribution. The channels

Figure 1.1
Major Marketing Channels for U.S. Grocery Products

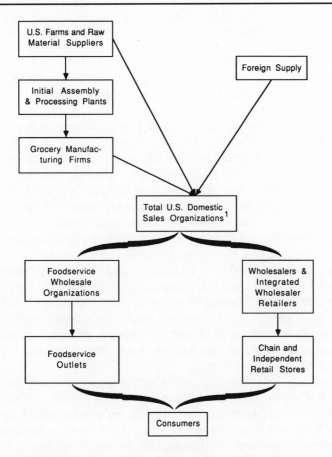

[1]Food manufacturing sales representatives, fresh food shipping organizations, and food brokers.

depicted account for approximately 98 percent of all grocery product distribution. "Grocery products" includes all products normally found in contemporary supermarkets: food and low-priced nonfood consumer goods such as health and beauty aids and general merchandise. The total supply of grocery products available for sale by domestic sales organizations originates from three sources: U.S. farms (e.g., fresh fruits, vegetables, fish, and eggs), foreign sources via U.S. import firms, and, most important, grocery product manufacturers. Approximately 75 percent of all grocery products come from the last manufacturing sector. These supplies pass through wholesalers and are distributed to consumers through various retail outlets – either food service (e.g., restaurants, cafeterias, airlines) or supermarket (e.g., corporate chain and independent stores) organizations. In 1989 the U.S. Department of Agriculture estimated that of the $514.9 billion spent on food by U.S. consumers, approximately 54 percent was spent in the various types of retail outlets primarily for consumption in the home. The other 46 percent was spent for away-from-home meals. This is a drastic change from several decades ago. In 1965, for example, 70 percent of all food was purchased in retail outlets for at-home consumption (USDA, 1990).

Consumers, at the receiving end of the marketing channel, are the driving force behind nearly all that happens upstream in the flow of goods and services. It is, after all, in an effort to satisfy consumers' wants and needs that the marketing system exists. The capricious and ever-changing consumer is responsible for and shapes many of the changes in the distribution system; thus, although often not considered as such, consumers should be viewed just as much as full-fledged participants in the distribution system as their upstream business enterprises. In fact, it is this new recognition of the importance of monitoring consumer change that has increasingly prompted businesses to elevate the status of their consumer research function to a critical part of their marketing strategies process. New consumer interests in healthy, low calorie, and convenient foods, for example, have been responsible for a number of marketing channel changes – in particular, the types and variety of new food products developed and introduced into the distribution system.

The new product planning, introduction processes, and buying and selling that are the subjects at hand here deal with only a portion of the channel stages of Figure 1.1. Specifically, we will focus here on the new product activities from the perspective of the manufacturer-seller and the supermarket-buyer. Although the remainder of the distribution system obviously influences our isolated segment of the channels – for example, our discussion of consumers – we do not address their activities further. It is abundantly clear that the manufacturer-supermarket interface remains dominant in terms of numbers of new products, systemwide costs, advertising activity, and people involved. Attention to this segment of the system possesses the greatest opportunity for improvements in both systemwide and firm-level performance.

MARKETING CHANNEL ORGANIZATION: MANUFACTURERS AND DISTRIBUTORS

Before attempting to investigate the behavior (conduct) or strategies of firms in the grocery distribution system (discussed in detail in Chapter 2), an understanding of the structure and organization of the system is required. Below, structural descriptions are developed along approximately similar criteria for both manufacturers and retailers.

Manufacturers

Food and tobacco manufacturing is an enormous industry.[1] In recent years, it has typically ranked third in gross value-added among the nineteen major industry groups of manufacturing, after transportation equipment and nonelectrical machinery (Census of Manufacturers, 1982). Although value-added is generally considered the best measure of the relative size of industries, food is the largest of manufacturing industries when calculated from a value-of-shipments basis. In 1982 shipments totaled $297 billion, or 14 percent of all manufacturing.

Among the various criteria generally employed to describe the structure of an industry, the number and size distribution of its firms, product differentiation, and entry barriers are most common. Also important are mergers and diversification.

Number and Size Distribution. The food manufacturing industry is characterized by a great many firms, the majority of them relatively small. Of the more than 20,000 establishments and companies that were primarily classified in food manufacturing in 1982 by the Bureau of Census, over half had fewer than ten employees and over 90 percent had fewer than one hundred employees.

On the other hand, a comparatively small number of large companies often exert influence far greater than their numbers would indicate. An important theme in industrial organization economics is that the fewer the number of companies in a given market (sometimes referred to as a horizontal industry), the greater is the likelihood that these companies will be able to gain market power and influence the quantity they produce, as well as the price and variety offered. This tendency is often best measured by concentration ratios. A concentration ratio expresses the percentage of the sales in a given market (how the market is defined is critical, of course) that is controlled by a certain number of firms. CR-4, CR-8, CR-12, and CR-20 are among the most common levels used for measuring the concentration of sales accounted for by four firms, eight firms, twelve firms, and twenty firms, respectively.

Average seller concentration among food and tobacco manufacturers has increased over time. In 1977 shipments from product classes in which the top four firms held less than 50 percent of shipments approximately equaled the shipments of product classes with CR-4 >50 percent (Marion, 1986, Table 4.1, p. 212). Since 1982, although all the data are not available, it appears probable that increases in concentration have continued to intensify due to the considerable number of mergers and acquisitions that have occurred in the food industry since that time.

From 1958 to 1977 the CR-4 increased 4 percentage points (or 9 percent) for eighty-five comparably defined food-tobacco product classes. On average, however, considerable differences emerge when concentration is examined by advertising intensity. In product classes where little or no media advertising (measured here by advertising-sales ratios) was reported, concentration actually decreased over the twenty-year period, while in groups where media advertising was medium to high, the CR-4 was significant. The weighted CR-4 in 1977 for the high-advertising category was 70.2 percent, about twice the level of the un-advertised and low-advertised groups. Generally, once the four-firm concentration ratio rises above about 40 percent, economists become wary of these few relatively large firms' negatively affecting the performance of the entire industry by such tactics as deliberately holding product off the market so as to raise overall price levels and engaging in other activities of sometimes questionable social value, such as promotional activities and perhaps needless product proliferation.

George J. Stigler and F. M. Scherer (Marion, 1986, p. 213) suggest that a 40 percent market share in a single firm may be adequate to confer price leadership on this firm. This can lead to collusive price coordination by eliminating the need for explicit agreements.

Although data on individual firm market share are rarely publicly available, John M. Conner (1985) examined 378 product categories in 1980 for the Nielsen Early Intelligence System (NEIS). Although these narrowly defined product categories are likely to overstate actual market share, nevertheless, the data show that the single leading brand held over 40 percent of category share in 204 of the 378 NEIS product categories. In 39 categories, private label brands as a group held over 40 percent of sales. In the remainder neither a single brand nor the private label group held a dominant position.

One industry that researchers and some public policy makers often cite as having a structure concentrated enough to carry with it many of the negative characteristics associated with theoretically concentrated industries is the cold cereal, or ready-to-eat cereal, industry. Breakfast cereals have been the second most concentrated of all food manufacturing industries for over forty years, exceeded only by chewing gum. Although in 1989 for the first time, Kellogg, the industry market share leader, had its portion of industry sales erode below the 40 percent level, the leading four firms still accounted for approximately 83.9 percent of all industry sales (Table 1.1). Furthermore, considerable evidence shows that these firms are very profitable. In 1988 the average return on equity for all manufacturing industries was 16.4 percent; for Kellogg, General Mills, and Ralston Purina, it was 34.1 percent, 36.2

Table 1.1
Cold Cereal Industry Market Shares

	1987	1988	1989
	- Percent of Sales -		
KELLOGG	42.0	42.2	39.6
GENERAL MILLS	23.6	24.4	26.5
GENERAL FOODS `	12.1	11.4	10.0
QUAKER OATS	7.9	8.0	7.8
RALSTON PURINA	6.1	5.9	6.6
NABISCO	4.9	4.8	4.5
OTHERS	3.4	3.3	5.0
TOTAL	100.0%	100.0%	100.0%

Source: Advertising Age, July 23, 1990.

percent, and 39.4 percent, respectively. Finally, these firms are heavy advertisers. While breakfast cereals accounted for only 2 percent of food industry shipments in 1987, they accounted for over 12 percent of all advertising expenditures on processed food.

Product Differentiation. A second dimension of industry structure generally thought to have an important impact on the behavior and specific strategies of industries and firms is product differentiation, defined as the degree to which the offerings of competing firms are perfect substitutes. Firms in a perfectly competitive world sell identical, homogeneous products, said to be undifferentiated. (Sometimes these are called commodities or generic products.) In the real world, managers generally work hard to differentiate their offerings from those of competitors in order to gain some sort of competitive advantage in the marketplace. Products that have been successfully differentiated from competing products usually become associated with a particular brand. Generally the more highly differentiated the brand is, the higher is its price premium in the marketplace.

Although physical differences are desirable in order to differentiate a product, they are not always necessary. Much of differentiation rests on imagery. Indeed, advertising is one of the major ways by which brands are differentiated. It is often used by researchers as a proxy for differentiation since the latter is difficult to measure directly. Manufactured food products possess several characteristics that aid advertising

(Greer, 1980; Porter, 1976, in Marion, 1986, p. 214). They are bought frequently, sold with relatively low unit prices, and are most often self-service. All these attributes tend to reinforce brand recognition and loyalty among consumers.

In 1988, according to *Advertising Age* (Sept. 24, 1989, p. 6), the measured expenditures on the advertising of supermarket-type products, excluding beer, wine, and health and beauty care products, exceeded $6 billion. This was higher than any other broad manufacturing category and has been since at least 1954. Measured advertising, however, includes only the ten media vehicles listed in Table 1.2. Unmeasured advertising, encompassing direct mail, promotion, co-operative advertising, couponing, catalogs, and miscellaneous special events, is not included but is estimated by *Advertising Age* to be more than twice as great as measured advertising. In 1988, for example, all advertisers spent $37,835.5 million on the ten media that were measured and $80,214.5 million more on advertising forms that were estimated from various sources, such as industry and company reports and spending trends. If this same approximate ratio holds for the grocery products industry as for the economy as a whole, we can estimate that total advertising, measured and unmeasured, by grocery product manufacturers was approximately $19,672 million.

Mass media is the main vehicle for this advertising, with television dominant in that regard. Table 1.2 shows the desegregated media expenditures for the six major media categories in 1988. Television, measured in all its current forms—network, spot, syndicated, and cable—accounts for over 80 percent of total expenditures on supermarket products, when tobacco products (for which television advertising is not permitted) are excluded. This is significant for two reasons. First, television is widely believed to be more effective than printed media in creating lasting impressions conducive to establishing and maintaining product differentiation (Porter, in Marion, 1976, p. 214), and, second, it tends to confer price discounts to large (firm) buyers (Levmore, Rogers, in Marion, 1976, p. 214). Significantly, the product classes that are the more intensive users of media advertising tend to be the most concentrated. The best examples are chewing gum, breakfast cereals, ready-to-mix desserts, and cigarettes; however, one must exercise caution in drawing conclusions too hastily from these observations. It is also true that a few of the most concentrated product classes, such as jarred baby food, have relatively low advertising-sales ratios. Jarred baby food has an advertising spending/sales ratio of 1.4, which may be considered quite modest in the face of a 6.7 ratio for all food products (*Advertising Age*, August 13, 1990). Whether this is due to the fact that firms with products in such very highly concentrated classes are able to maintain dominance and forestall new entrants with

Table 1.2
National Measured Media Expenditures for Grocery Products, by Category, 1988

Category	Total Spending Million $	--Percent--									
		Magazines	Newspaper Supplements	Newspaper	Outdoor	Network TV	Spot TV	Syndicated TV	Cable TV	Network Radio	Spot Radio
Food	3655.9	10.30	0.01	1.30	0.01	43.00	25.10	6.20	2.40	2.10	8.40
Snacks & Soft Drinks	1173.5	4.30	0.01	0.01	0.01	42.00	31.60	8.50	3.40	3.40	4.80
Cigarettes & Tobacco	656.3	53.60	7.60	8.40	28.10	0.00	0.01	0.00	0.00	0.01	0.00
Soaps & Cleaners	572.8	8.80	0.00	0.00	0.00	54.10	22.90	7.20	3.70	0.01	0.02
Pet Foods	12.6	12.60	0.00	0.02	0.00	51.30	17.10	9.60	3.80	2.70	0.01
Total	6305.5										

[1] Unmeasured media and promotional spending not included.

[2] Beer, wine & liquor excluded.

[3] Includes minor expenditures for pets.

Note: Excludes unmeasured media and promotional spending and beer, wine and liquor. Only minor expenditures for pets are included.

Source: Advertising Age, September 27, 1989.

comparatively low advertising or to other more complex nonlinear relationships requires further study.

Advertising expenditures are highly concentrated among a relatively small number of very large firms. In 1982, 81.5 percent of all media advertising originated from the 50 largest food advertisers from the over 1,100 companies for which media expenditures were measured. The twelve largest advertisers accounted for 45 percent of the total, a gain from their 40 percent share in 1967.

In 1988, Philip Morris, the largest grocery products company in the United States, became the first company to lavish $2 billion in annual advertising and promotional spending in the United States, with an increase of 7.2 percent to $2.06 billion (Table 1.3). The company's recently acquired Kraft General Foods division, with combined sales of $22.5 billion, accounted for about 60 percent of Philip Morris' total advertising expenditures. Table 1.3 also shows that Procter & Gamble, another of the nation's leading grocery products companies, is second on the list of the top national advertisers, spending $1.5 billion in 1988. In fact, it was the dominant spender until it was edged out by Philip Morris in 1987. Of the leading spenders in 1988, seven of the top ten were grocery or food companies; only General Motors, Sears, Roebuck & Co., and Eastman Kodak were not.

Table 1.3
Expenditures for Top Ten National Advertisers, 1988

Rank	Advertiser	Spending Total --Million $--
1	Philip Morris Cos	2,058.2
2	Procter & Gamble Co.	1,506.9
3	General Motors Corp.	1,294.0
4	Sears, Roebuck & Co.	1,045.2
5	RJR Nabisco	814.5
6	Grand Met PLC	773.9
7	Eastman Kodak Co.	735.9
8	McDonalds Corp.	728.3
9	PepsiCo Inc.	712.3
10	Kellogg Co.	683.1

Note: Expenditures are measured and unmeasured.

Source: Advertising Age, November 27, 1989.

There is some recent indication, however, that consumer advertising by all food firms may be reversing its long-term rise. For the first nine months of 1989, total food manufacturer advertising spending in nine major media categories (network, spot cable and syndicated television, network and spot radio, billboard, magazines, and Sunday supplements) declined by 3.4 percent compared to year-earlier levels (USDA, May 1990). This decline is believed to reflect a drop in advertising throughout the economy and some scaling down in expenditures as a result of mergers and leveraged buyouts.

Concentration levels are even higher when television advertising is considered alone (Rogers and Mather, in Marion, 1976, p. 215). In 1982, twelve firms accounted for 59 percent of network advertising of food, and the top fifty television food advertisers held 95.5 percent of network advertising. This clearly shows the advertising dominance and potential influence of the top food advertisers as they attempt to build sales and profits through brand differentiation.

Media advertising constitutes one of the most critical ways in which manufacturers attempt to create differentiation and solidify their brand positions, but it is generally only a small portion of the total advertising and promotional activities of the firm. Advertising and promotional monies are often divided into categories depending on their push or pull properties. Push advertising is designed to push the product through the grocery system primarily by providing incentives for wholesalers and retailers to stock and sell the item. Pull advertising is targeted toward consumers, who, it is believed, will respond to the advertising by demanding the products from their respective retail outlets and thus pull it through the system. Much push promotion is difficult to classify and measure (e.g., advertising in trade journals); some manufacturer selling costs are inaccessible (e.g., certain "trade development funds" like slotting allowances, and expenditures for some promotional activities such as consumer coupons, contests, and trade shows) and do not appear in the media.

Figure 1.2 shows that in 1987, the latest year for which these data are available, only about one-third of overall advertising and promotional budgets of all manufacturers was devoted to advertising. Moreover, this amount has been decreasing over time in both absolute and in relative terms. In 1977, for example, activities classified as advertising constituted 41 percent of total promotional monies (sales promotion and advertising), whereas in 1987 these activities represented only 35 percent. Yet the absolute amount of total promotional spending rose over that same period an astonishing amount: from $56.2 billion to $171.8 billion.

Four main factors account for this gradual shift from advertising to promotion:

Figure 1.2
Advertising and Promotion Spending ($ in billions)

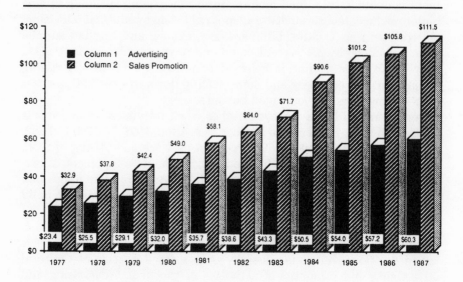

Source: Marketing Communications (August 1988).

1. Increasingly competitive markets in all industries have led to a greater emphasis on measurable results at the bottom line, a change reflecting the new corporate emphasis on financial accountability. Promotional activities are able to be gauged more accurately regarding their impact on sales performance. Their impacts are more easily measurable than those of advertising.

2. The growing concentration of the wholesale and retail trade has resulted in increasing pressure on suppliers to produce short-term merchandising events, favored by retailers for their ability to create consumer excitement. Scanner data and space management systems have permitted retailers to become more sophisticated in their evaluation of promotional programs, and, moreover, retailers have provided manufacturers with convincing evidence that sales performance can increase with the correct combination of manufacturer-retailer support.

3. In many slow-growth markets, manufacturers are under pressure to produce continuous movement and growth, often quarterly. Promotional events, even if perhaps not profitable in the long run, do result in temporary volume increases.

4. The decline in national media (especially television) penetration has increased all efforts at local and regional marketing activity, including individual-store-level promotional spending. Given the continued decline in mass marketing approaches, it appears likely that these shifts will continue.

Barriers to Entry. A final structural index serving to describe an industry is barriers to entry, defined as anything that prevents an outside firm from entering into an otherwise attractive industry. Although established firms have a self-interest in erecting barriers to entry to protect their established territories and brands, some economists argue that such barriers allow entrenched firms to become lazy, to lose their competitive edge to be innovative, and to operate at less than low-cost production. Hence, industry performance becomes nonoptimal, and consumers may end up paying higher-than-necessary prices for inferior-quality merchandise. Some commonly considered barriers to entry are economies of scale, product differentiation, and absolute cost advantages. The evidence for the extent and the height of entry barriers in food manufacturing is mixed.

Several studies suggest that plant economies of scale are not substantial in food manufacturing. The average U.S. food manufacturing industry could accommodate approximately thirty-five to fifty efficient-sized plants (Marion, 1976, p. 218), a size small enough not to present insurmountable barriers to potential entrants. Less is known, however, about the multiplant or firm-level economics of size (lower production and distribution costs) that may exist for certain very large firms. Economics here are likely to result from conglomerate cross-subsidization of activities, discounts that may result from volume purchasing such as advertising, and generally greater control and bargaining leverage enjoyed because of greater size and power in the distribution system. The few studies that have been conducted have concluded that multiplant economics of size are probably realized with 5 to 10 percent of the market or a CR-4 of 40 percent or less.

Product differentiation can be an especially steep barrier in the branded segment of food manufacturing. Not only is the advertising effectiveness of new entrants likely to be less than that of established firms due to the familiarity of the brand(s) of the latter, but there is also some evidence of increasing marginal returns to advertising, essentially for the same reason: small firms would have to launch an enormously expensive advertising campaign in order to break through what may be described as consumers' recognition threshold in the prevailing climate of advertising clutter. Small and medium-sized firms, often struggling to build and maintain business, cannot countenance the size of the advertising budget necessary. In addition, access to prime time, the evening hours with the largest television audience, is generally reserved for the large advertisers, who are allocated these desirable slots as part of their much larger total advertising program.

Finally, there are a host of potential entry barriers as a result of the absolute size of an incumbent firm, generally the case with multiproduct and multimarket firms. Specifically, large firms, as a result of their often numerous product lines and multiple geographical markets, are able to engage in strategies that discourage entry of new firms that a smaller, single-line firm could not. Established firms can lower prices to levels that could not be endured by a new entrant struggling to survive; the incumbent simply cross-subsidizes these temporary losses with profits earned from other product lines or from different geographical markets.

One may draw some cautious conclusions from this discussion of entry barriers into food manufacturing. In general, most research studies have not found strong evidence of economies of scale or size in food manufacturing (Marion, 1986). Entry into the producer (e.g., commodity), unbranded, and private label food business does not appear to be inhibited by unreasonable barriers. In the branded food business, however, it appears safe to conclude that product differentiation caused in important part by manufacturers' massive advertising campaigns is a considerable deterrent to entry by small firms. Otherwise, some researchers reason indirectly, why are there so many industries where there exists a significant positive statistical relationship between profits and concentration? If these highly concentrated industries did not somehow present entry barriers, the usual expectation would be that new firms would be attracted to the high level of profits. However, there are a considerable number of industries where concentration and advertising levels are quite high yet new entrants have been few: breakfast cereals, chewing gum, cigarettes, coffee, beer, and soft drinks.

Diversification. A number of types of diversification, or integration, are relevant to the structure of food manufacturing: horizontal, vertical, and conglomerate. Horizontal diversification refers to the lateral shift of a manufacturer, or any firm, into an adjacent line of business with similar production processes or marketing systems (e.g., a soft drink manufacturer that begins to produce fruit juice products). Vertical diversification describes the condition whereby a manufacturer becomes engaged in the input supply stages of the industry or in the distribution of final finished products (e.g., a manufacturer opens retail stores). Conglomerate diversification occurs when a manufacturer owns product lines that are neither horizontally or vertically related to its own industry (e.g., a manufacturer of frozen vegetables invests in an automobile tire plant).

Measurement problems prevent us from being precise with respect to the extent of diversification in the food industry. Many of the required data are proprietary, and even the best public data are somewhat arbitrary and blurred as a result of the necessary classification of firms according to their primary and secondary activity. In many of the most diversified food manufacturing firms, for example, the primary business may account for less than 10 percent of overall business. Nonetheless, some useful information may be presented describing the structural diversity of food manufacturing. In a 1983 study by James M. MacDonald cited by Marion (1976, p. 233), approximately 44 percent of the nonfood manufacturing sales (conglomerate diversification) of seventy-two manufacturers with food as their primary industry was in chemicals. Other findings of interest from these same data were the vertical integration into containers (plastics, paper, can, and glass) and food machinery; conglomerate diversification into other consumer products such as apparel, furniture, and games; and little diversification into industrial products. Slightly over half (53 percent) of the food manufacturers had significant sales in wholesaling and retailing.

Moreover, John M. Conner and Loys L. Mather (Marion, 1976) identified 38 firms whose main business was classified outside the food industry but whose total sales in the food industry resulted in their being among the 200 largest food and tobacco companies in 1975. Of the 38, 18 were in other manufacturing industries, such as soap and drugs, 8 were wholesalers, and 7 were food retailers. On average in 1977, 31 percent of food and tobacco sales were by companies classified primarily outside the principal enterprise category.

Vertical diversification, or integration, in food manufacturing can be backward or forward. For the largest 500 food and tobacco manufacturers between 1967 and 1977, backward vertical integration into input supply manufacturing accounted for about 3 percent of total payroll, whereas forward diversification into a range of transportation, wholesaling, and retailing industries involved in handling of food accounted for approximately 20 percent of payroll, although declining somewhat over the period. Of this latter figure, the most important part – 15.2 percent – goes to retail stores. During this same ten years, conglomerate diversification rose by 23 percent by 1977, accounting for 39 percent of company payroll (Marion, 1986).

Mergers. Related to diversification is merger activity, which has become an increasingly dominant factor in attempting to explain the structure of the contemporary food system. Indeed, the high levels of all types of diversification are partially explained by the ease with which firms are often able to acquire, rather than build, new assets. Although antitrust provisions prohibit certain kinds of horizontal mergers, they rarely pertain to vertical or conglomerate mergers. Following a relatively stable period during the 1970s, the 1980s was marked by a period of intensive merger activity. For example, "relative to the total amount of assets potentially available to be acquired, on average about 0.8 percent of food manufacturer assets were actually acquired per year during 1948-1980; during 1981-1984 (alone) that proportion rose to 2.7 percent" (Marion, 1986, p. 240).

Changing structure was one of the dominant issues in the U.S. food system throughout the 1980s. Between 1982 and 1988, the years for which the Economic Research Service of the U.S. Department of Agriculture monitored these trends, nearly 3,400 mergers, divestitures, or leveraged buyouts took place in food marketing firms. Food manufacturing, which had 16,800 companies in 1982, had more than 2,000 of these transactions.

In the mid-1980s the merger, acquisition, and divestiture pace continued to gain momentum, but there is preliminary evidence that the trend may be changing. In 1986 continued consolidation and restructuring of the food industry produced 724 industry-related mergers and acquisitions, the highest number on record for the decade, according to the Food Institute (*Marketing News*, 1987). During that year the merger activity was 10 percent greater than the 658 recorded in 1985 and 9 percent above the previous record of 666 in 1981. There were 114 merger transactions recorded by food processing firms compared to only 95 the year earlier.

By the end of the 1980s, however, several countertrends were evident. Although the number of merges and acquisitions in the food processing and manufacturing industry continued to grow in 1988 (to 136), they fell to 107 in 1989. Similarly, the number of mergers and acquisitions in the entire food industry fell from mid-1980s levels to 652 in 1988 and then to 556 in 1989 (Table 1.4). Transactions dropped not only in number but also in dollar magnitude.

This recent decline is not surprising given that the earlier frenzied pace of merger activity certainly reduced the number of likely merger and leveraged buyout candidates that remained. More significant, however, the high-yield, high-risk ("junk") bond market sharply weakened toward the end of 1989, drying up a major source of financing. Further, financial institutions appeared more reluctant to provide financing. The vast proportion of acquisitions of food processing firms came from firms outside the food industry (Table 1.4), and in 1988, twenty-two foreign buyers bought U.S. food processing companies with a combined value of $8.6 billion (Gallo, 1990).

This increase in mergers has had a predictable effect on food manufacturing concentration. Aggregate concentration in food manufacturing, wholesaling, and foodservice firms rose in 1989. The top three food manufacturing firms' share of market grew from 9.5 percent to 13 percent between 1988 and 1989. In 1989, the largest leveraged buyout in U.S. history occurred: Kohlberg Kravis Roberts and Co. acquired RJR Nabisco for $24.72 billion. This transaction exceeded the combined value of history's five largest food marketing mergers. In 1988 the acquisition leaders in food manufacturing were Borden, Kraft, Inc., Conagra, Inc., IC Industries, Inc., and H. J. Heinz Company.

Table 1.4
Food Business Mergers and Acquisitions, 1988 and 1989

Category	Total Acquisitions		Individual Purchasers	Acquisitions of Firms Outside Food Industry
	Number			
	1989	1988		
Agricultural cooperatives	4	5	4	1
Bakers	27	19	18	0
Brewers	3	1	2	1
Brokers	14	11	14	0
Confectioners	10	12	9	0
Dairy processors	14	19	10	14
Diversified firms with interests in the food industry	4	31	1	0
Food processing firms	107	136	5	66
Foodservice vendors	29	31	23	1
Hotel and lodging companies	6	1	5	NA
Nonfood marketers selling through supermarkets	7	7	6	NA
Packaging suppliers	25	27	17	NA
Poultry processors	5	7	5	0
Primary products companies	47	18	40	5
Restaurant and foodservice concerns	57	74	54	1
Retailers:				
Convenience stores	16	18	15	0
Supermarkets	26	42	25	0
Others	9	13	8	6
Seafood processors	4	5	3	0
Snack food processors	6	12	6	0
Soft drink bottlers	12	18	7	0
Sugar refiners	1	0	1	0
Suppliers to the food industry	3	9	3	NA
Unclassified and private investors	21	30	21	3
Wholesalers	21	29	20	0
Foreign acquisitions:				
U.S. firms/subsidiaries	55	29	54	11
U.S. operators of foreign firms	4	6	4	1
Foreign operators of U.S. firms	6	8	6	2
By Canadian firms	10	14	10	0
Total	556	652	459	52

Source: Gallo (1990).

Retailers

Number and Size Distribution. Grocery retailers (that is, distributors of food and nonfood consumer nondurables) receive their merchandise from various grocery manufacturers via some form of integrated grocery wholesaler-retailer. The term *integrated* is used to draw attention to the evolution of the modern grocery company. Earlier in this century, a clear distinction could be drawn between the retail level of the grocery distribution, where grocers met shoppers in the retail shop, and the wholesale level, where the procurement, storage, and physical handling and local transportation of merchandise took place.

The advent of the chain type of grocery organization in the 1920s and 1930s, where the wholesale function was fused together as one corporate entity with the retail level, led to significant economies in purchasing and operations and to other competitive advantages not then enjoyed by the independent wholesalers and retailers. As a result of the rapid growth of retail chains, vertical integration began between wholesalers and retailers — not in the form of corporate ownership but rather other types of contractual integration, such as voluntary and cooperative buying organizations. In 1988 approximately 92.2 percent of grocery sales were accounted for by one of the various forms of chains or affiliated (voluntary or cooperative) wholesaler (Table 1.5). Convenience stores, a growing industry segment, accounted for 7.8 percent of grocery store sales in 1988. Retailers not affiliated with a major wholesaler now account for so little (only a few percentage points) of all retail food sales that their sales figures are no longer officially reported. Although the retailers affiliated with one of the principal wholesalers remain independent in name, they generally depend equally as much as the retail chain on the central wholesale facility for virtually all types of operational and competitive support. Thus, the former distinction between the wholesale and retail level in the grocery industry has now become blurred to an important degree. For this reason, the term *retailer* will be used here to refer to the functions performed at both levels of the system. Moreover, recognizing this new industry reality, grocery manufacturers do not themselves generally make a distinction between the two firm types: all buyers, in the trade jargon, are simply retailers.

Marion (1986, p. 297) points to several noteworthy trends with respect to the structure of grocery retailing. First, for more than thirty years, there has been a near secular decline in the number of outlets, while these fewer outlets account for a greater volume of sales in real terms. This phenomenon is explained by the larger individual outlets and the much broader product mix that has become the industry norm. Second, although specialty food stores connote high-quality products and service in many countries, they also have continued to lose sales to their much larger counterparts for the better part of five decades. In

Table 1.5
Grocery Store Sales, by Size and Ownership, 1988

	# of stores	% of total	$ sales (millions)	% of total
All stores	148,000	100.0	329,000	100.0
Supermarkets (over $2.0 mil.)	30,400	20.5	240,000	73.0
Independent supermarkets ($ mil.)	13,550	9.1	78,100	23.1
$2 – 3.9	6,670	4.5	19,700	6.0
$4 – 7.9	4,470	3.0	24,500	7.4
$8 – 11.9	1,200	0.8	11,600	3.5
$12 and over	1,210	0.8	20,300	8.2
Chain supermarkets ($ millions)	18,850	11.4	184,300	49.9
$2 – 3.9	1,705	1.2	5,100	1.5
$4 – 7.9	5,655	3.8	33,900	10.3
$8 – 11.9	4,410	3.0	44,000	13.4
$12 and over	5,080	3.4	81,300	24.7
Convenience Stores[1]	55,000	37.2	25,500	7.8
Other Stores (under $2 mil.)	62,600	42.3	63,100	19.2
By affiliation				
Independent	75,800	51.2	139,200	42.3
Chain	17,200	11.6	164,300	49.9
Convenience store[1]	55,000	37.2	25,500	7.8
By supermarket format, total	30,400	100.0	240,400	100.0
Conventional	20,940	68.9	120,400	50.1
Extended	6,050	19.9	83,200	34.6
Economy[2]	3,410	11.2	36,800	15.3

[1]Excludes sales of gasoline.
[2]Includes limited assortment, warehouse, super warehouse, and hypermarket.

Source: Progressive Grocer's Annual Report of the Grocery Industry, 1989.

the 1930s, specialty stores (e.g., bakeries, greengrocers, butcher shops) did about 30 percent of all food store sales, a figure that declined to 6 percent in 1982. Finally, there has been an inexorable increase in chain store sales at the expense of independents.

Concentration. Most economists agree that while national concentration statistics on grocery retailers can shed light on certain characteristics of the industry (e.g., buying power and likelihood of potential entrants), it is not as useful a structural measure for grocery retailers as it is for manufacturers. The reason is fundamental: manufactured grocery products are sold to distributors on a national market but to consumers on local markets. The buyers of retail organizations can search on the national market for an alternative supplier if they are dissatisfied with their current supply source; consumers cannot. Consumers do not travel widely to shop. Many surveys show that for most store types, supermarket customers travel fewer than 2 miles for their groceries. This means that the consumer trading area is generally quite small relative to the overall size of the market.

Consequently, when describing the structure of grocery retailing, it is important to examine not only the national concentration picture but the local market conditions as well. Beginning in about 1977, the intensity of the merger and acquisition activity was considerably greater in the grocery retailing industry than it was in the manufacturing sector. The acquisitions of grocery retailers, including leveraged buyouts, by all other firm types increased measurably over the past four decades. By the end of 1987, eight of the top twenty supermarket chains were private (*Supermarket News*, January 11, 1988). Table 1.6 lists those companies. The same companies, with only a few exceptions, retained their positions in 1989–90.

During the 1980s, several mergers of unprecedented size took place. The Kroger Company acquired the Dillon Company in 1983, and the operator of Alpha Beta supermarkets acquired Jewel in 1984. Toward the end of the decade, it appeared as if the pace was first accelerating,

Table 1.6
Leading Supermarket Chains, 1987

Rank	Company	1987 Sales (000 omitted)
1	Safeway	$18,300,000
2	Kroger	17,660,000
3	American Stores	14,272,000
4	A & P	9,532,000
5	Winn-Dixie Stores	9,008,000
6	Lucky Stores	6,440,000
7	Albertson's	5,869,000
8	Supermarkets General	5,800,000
9	Stop & Shop	4,300,000
10	Publix	4,100,000
11	Vons	3,200,000
12	Grand Union	2,746,000
13	Food Lion	2,407,000
14	Ralphs	2,000,000
15	H.E. Butt	2,000,000
16	Dominick's	1,740,000
17	Fred Meyer	1,700,000
18	First National	1,500,000
19	Giant Eagle	1,400,000
20	Hy-Vee Food Stores	1,400,000

Source: Annual reports.

then beginning to decline, in parallel fashion with manufacturers. For 1988–89, forty-two individual mergers and acquisitions took place for supermarket companies; this number fell to twenty-six in 1989 (Table 1.4). In 1988, American Stores was again active; it acquired Lucky Stores, making it the top volume food retailer in the United States. Also in 1988, Vons acquired Safeway's southern California stores, and K-Mart purchased a majority interest in Makro, a membership warehouse club store. All of these mergers have added to national levels of concentration. Table 1.7 illustrates the concentration levels for grocery chains from 1948 to 1987. Over this approximately forty years, the CR-4 declined marginally from 20.1 percent to 17.4 percent, while the CR-8 increased marginally from 23.7 percent to 26.5 percent. The marked difference, however, comes when the share of sales held by the top twenty firms is investigated. It increased from 26.9 percent in 1948 to 37.2 percent in 1987; or, when the former giant retailer, A&P, is excluded, the concentration level for the top twenty firms grew from 16.2 percent in 1948 to 36.1 percent in 1986 – a 122 percent increase.

Such national concentration numbers do not give us much insight into how groceries are sold on the local market. For this, we need to know how much of the sales in the relevant local market are held by the top group of companies. Unfortunately, statistics defining the relevant market do not exist. Instead, most analysts rely on a statistical area defined by the Bureau of Census as Metropolitan Statistical Areas (MSA), although in many instances these areas are thought to be much broader than the area in which most consumers are believed to confine

Table 1.7
Percentage Share of U.S. Grocery Store Sales Held by the Twenty Largest Grocery Chains, Census Years 1948–1987

Firm Size	1948	1954	1958	1963	1967	1972	1977	1982	1987
Four largest	20.1	20.9	21.7	20.0	19.0	17.5	17.4	17.8	17.4
Fifth to eight largest	3.6	4.5	5.8	6.6	6.7	6.9	7.0	7.3	9.1
Eight largest	23.7	25.4	27.5	26.6	25.7	24.4	24.4	25.1	26.5
Ninth to twentieth largest	3.2	4.5	6.6	7.4	8.7	10.4	10.1	10.4	10.7
Twenty largest	26.9	29.9	34.1	34.0	34.4	34.8	34.5	35.6	37.2

Source: Compiled from Census of Retail Trade, various years.

their shopping. Often several different major cities are included in one
MSA. Thus, if anything, using MSAs understates the actual concentration levels in relevant markets.

Concentration in the grocery retailing markets using MSAs has experienced a consistent upward trend since at least 1958 (Figure 1.3).
For the 173 that experienced no definitional change between 1958 and
1959, the average CR-4 increased from 48.7 to 58.6. Further, although
only 18 percent of the MSAs had CR-4s of 60 percent or greater in
1967, this figure had grown to 44 percent by 1982. Since a grocery store
CR-4 of 60 translates to a supermarket CR-4 of roughly 75, it can be
said that nearly half of U.S. metropolitan areas had very concentrated
grocery markets by 1982. Some indication exists, however, that after
reaching a CR-4 of 60 or so, there is a tendency for the increase to taper
off. It might be that once four firms become so dominant that they
together control 60 percent of all local grocery sales, gaining further
sales almost inevitably means taking them away from one of the already dominant top firms. Given what may be a fairly equitable distribution of competitive strengths, the likelihood that one of the top four
will gain further on keen competitors may be quite small.

These relatively high degrees of retailer concentration, at least at the
relevant local market level, are often a signal within the context of industrial organization theory that prices and profits in these markets
are likely to be higher than unconcentrated markets. However, a recent
study conducted by the Bureau of Economics at the Federal Trade
Commission (FTC) (1990) casts doubt on decades of grocery retailing
concentration studies. In essence, the FTC study concluded that there
are significant problems with specific aspects of the economic theory
and statistical methodology employed in many of the past studies on
concentration in grocery retailing and that the most recent study of
pricing and concentration in food retailing—which avoids only some of
the problems of earlier studies—finds no indication that prices are generally higher in concentrated markets. Thus, past work, much of which
points to violations of consumer welfare as a result of concentrated
markets, may not provide a sound basis for determining or proscribing
an appropriate merger or antitrust policy for grocery retailers.

Foreign Ownership. Over the 1980s, the consolidation of grocery
companies was promoted by a continued increase in foreign ownership.
Because of restricted expansion in many home markets and the vast
and seemingly attractive American consumer market, certain foreign
firms had looked to the United States for some time. However, the dollar's weakness combined with many declines in retail stock prices in the
late 1980s to stimulate interest. In 1988, Marks & Spencer, a dominant
retail chain in the United Kingdom, acquired Kings Super Markets in
New Jersey, adding to a growing number of foreign retailers with at

Figure 1.3
Distribution of 173 MSAs by Grocery Store Sales, Four-Firm Concentration Levels, Various Years

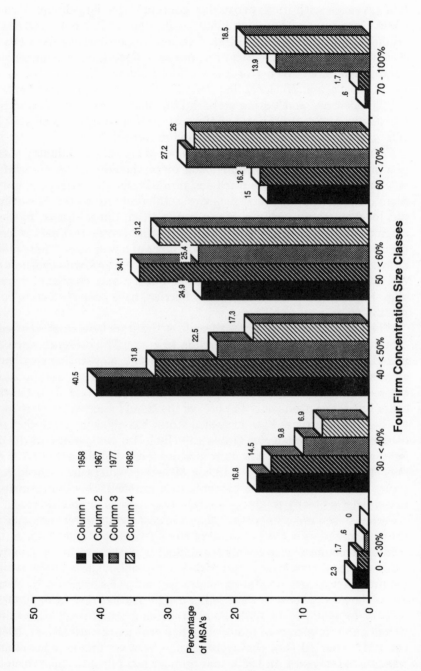

Source: Special tabulation of Census of Retail Trade, various years, reported in Marion (1988).

least some investment in the U.S. grocery system: Auchan and Carrefour (France), with its hypermarket concepts; the Tengelmann Group (West Germany), with its dominant position in A&P; Ahold (the Netherlands), owner of BI-LO, First National Supermarkets, and Giant (Pennsylvania); Delhaize (Belgium), owner of Food Lion; J. Sainsbury's (United Kingdom), owner of Shaw's; and Loblaws (Canada), owner of P. J. Schmitt and National Tea. In 1988 direct foreign investment in U.S. "foodstores" and "eating and drinking places" combined was $3 billion (Gallo, 1990). By the end of 1988, an estimated 10 to 15 percent of U.S. grocery company assets were foreign owned.

Entry Barriers. Although the existence of barriers to industry entry is a significant structural dimension often thought to be associated with higher than desirable price and profit levels, the concept is much more difficult to isolate and measure in the retailing sector. For example, local store ownership changes hands often. Large chains, in their attempts to upgrade existing stores and find better real estate locations, frequently spin off older units in favor of newer ones. These older stores are often repurchased by independent operators, who continue to make use of the capacity. This is not new entry, only change of ownership. However, several specific entry barriers have been studied in connection to grocery retailing.

Where significant economies of scale at the store level exist, they certainly would be indication of barriers to entry. The evidence appears mixed. Several studies examining the link between operating costs and store size found either modest or no significant statistical relationship between the two in the 1960s and 1970s (Marion, 1976, p. 313). On the other hand, one needs only to observe the trend in new store sizes over the last decade to see how large-size stores have become an important competitive tool to survive (Table 1.8). Table 1.8 also points up the dilemma for retail buyers: new store size has increased since the 1970s by only 47 percent, while the number of new products introduced has grown by a staggering 795 percent. In a nutshell, this is a principal reason that so many products are rejected; there is simply no room.

Perhaps even more important than the cost-reducing technologies in these large stores is the potential of these stores to attract huge numbers of consumers with their typically wide grocery aisles, expansive fresh service departments, and wide product mix. These larger stores require much larger capital expenditures and sales volumes to break even. The average cost of remodeling a supermarket rose from $63,600 in 1977 to $488,000 in 1988 (Food Marketing Institute, 1989). Additionally, the frequency of remodeling has grown dramatically. In 1980, the FMI reported that the average time between major remodelings was five to ten years. In 1989, that number had fallen to three to eight years. In 1989, the average age of a chain supermarket was 14.8 years,

Table 1.8
New Food Products and Retail Store Space, 1970–1989

	AVERAGE 1970-81	1987	1988	1989	1970/81-89 PERCENT CHANGE
NEW FOOD PRODUCTS	1,026	7,866	8,183	9,192	795%
NEW STORE SIZE (sq. ft.)	27,200	46,892	40,800	40,000	47%

Source: Gorman's New Product News (Gorman Publishing Company, 1990).

and the average age of a remodeling was 2.9 years (*Progressive Grocer,* April 1990).

More staggering is the cost of opening a new store: the average new supermarket in 1988 cost approximately $3.9 million in total construction costs, $1.3 million in equipment costs, and an additional $0.7 million for opening inventory (FMI, 1989; Standard and Poors, 1989). Furthermore, the considerable cost of a new lease must be added; it may range from $2 million to $7 million or $8 million per store, a cost that only the largest companies can afford.

Another group of barriers that may confront existing firms includes a range of activities and costs associated with multiple stores in a given market. These types of economies arise from such factors as the steep costs of advertising in a medium- or large-size market. A new entrant can expect to pay as much as 5 percent of sales for advertising during its first years of entry as opposed to the approximately 1 percent that established firms pay on average. A related economy is likely to exist with the more substantial trade advertising allowances that manufacturers offer to existing firms because of their much larger volume of business. Although the same relative discount, proportional to the smaller volume, may be available to the new entrant, the absolute advantage is likely to be much lower due to less impact per dollar of cost. It is reasonable to expect that store numbers must increase quickly if the new firm is to attain the same cost advantage as its established counterparts. Actual estimates of these potential barriers are not available, however.

A popular retailing adage is that "there are only three things important in retailing: location, location, location." Supermarkets must be built where there is, or will be, a high density of shoppers. This often means a shopping center. Yet shopping center developers want well-established firms with well-established reputations that are likely to help them attract the greatest numbers of shoppers to the center. The supermarket is often the anchor of the development. Most developers are loathe to take a risk on a new entrant into the grocery business. A new entrant is likely to succeed only if it agrees to pay a higher rent than would be necessary for a leading retail operator.

Finally, a group of strategic behaviors serves as potential entry barriers for which a reasonable argument can be marshaled but, again, for which little hard data exist to substantiate them. Included are tactics by incumbents such as zone pricing and increased advertising, followed by cross-subsidization of the temporary losses from other geographic markets. Similarly, some retailers often purposely create excess capacity to prevent access to new entrants to the preferred sites. They do this by buying select properties and holding them, often without immediate plans to develop the properties. All of these tactics raise the entrant's cost of business and may forestall or even prevent entry.

Marion (1986, p. 318) summarizes what has been learned about entry barriers into grocery retailing:

Entry barriers are clearly higher in large SMSAs (Standard Metropolitan Statistical Areas). All else the same, entry barriers are also higher in SMSAs in which a high percentage of grocery store sales are held by supermarkets indicating that there is little unmet demand for supermarkets; supermarket sales are highly concentrated; there is one or more dominant chain in the market; there are several multimarket regional or national chains that can subsidize strategic behavior in particular markets; and there is little or no growth in SMSA grocery store sales.

Finally, most statistical studies have found a significant positive relationship between concentration and profit in grocery retailing (Marion, 1986). For lack of better and more unequivocal measures of entry barriers, many economists reason indirectly that this relationship could not persist if entry barriers did not exist.

Retail Formats. Although most of the previous discussion treats all supermarkets as belonging to the same approximate competitive group, in fact, considerable splintering of store types occurred during the 1960s and 1970s. Before that time, retail grocery stores belonged more or less to the same homogeneous group, serving what may be described as the same mass, homogeneous consumer population. Increasing consumer demographic and life-style differences gave retailers the opportunity to differentiate themselves from their competitors by catering to these new consumer segments. New store formats were created.

In addition to the conventional supermarket formula, retailers added a variety of much larger stores, ranging from bare-bones, price-oriented warehouse stores, to superstores, superwarehouse stores, combination drug-grocery stores, and, largest of all, hypermarkets. Table 1.9 displays several key industry characteristics of a range of these supermarket formats at the end of the 1980s. The vast differences in operating characteristics of these different formats place them in quite different competitive circumstances and different strategic groups. The appearance of a variety of store formats has an important influence on industry structure since it changes the definition of competition. One could forcefully argue, for example, that although specialty stores and convenience stores are both important grocery outlets, neither really competes for the same consumers as their larger counterparts that provide the breadth of assortment and price levels for consumers' major shopping trips. This is particularly true of the petroleum-based gas station–convenience store category. Table 1.9 indicates the increasing numbers and greater total market share controlled by the range of the larger store formats, generally at the expense of the conventional store. Whereas the conventional supermarket controlled the majority (55.2 percent) of all supermarket sales in 1980, it is forecast to account for only 24.9 percent of the market by 1994. During the same period, superstores, food-drug combo stores, warehouse stores, and other expanded formats have captured the conventional store loss. Moreover, these larger store formats are projected by most industry analysts to continue to erode the sales of the conventional store types in the future.

Vertical Integration. Grocery retailers and wholesalers have tended to integrate their activities into the same vertical system, either by ownership or other contractual control, so as to render the former distinction between these two firm types unclear—hence, the term *integrated wholesaler-retailer.* Some of these integrated wholesaler-retailers have extended their activities backward into various forms of commodity handling, transportation, initial food processing, and private label food manufacturing. Most of the food manufacturing by retail grocery companies is done by the largest companies. Between 1954 and 1967, the percentage of food sales of the largest forty chains supplied by their own manufacturing plants declined and then, after 1967 and 1977, grew slightly (Marion, 1986, p. 336). Manufacturing by the chains smaller than the leading forty is relatively unimportant. Of those foods most often supplied by retailers' own manufacturing plants, fluid milk, fresh and processed meats, and bread accounted for two-thirds of the value of manufactured food by the largest fifty chains in 1977.

Although the data necessary to study this question are not available, the fact that many of the largest companies still maintain some food manufacturing capacity, and a few are actually engaged in considerable food manufacturing, suggests that some benefits exist to this type of vertical integration. Whether these benefits are in the form of econo-

Table 1.9
Retail Formats and Selected Characteristics, 1990

| | A. STORE CHARACTERISTICS | | | B. GROWTH TRENDS | | | | | |
| | | | | 1980 | | 1989 | | 1994 | |
	Total Area (Sq.Ft.)	Weekly Sales	# of Items	# of Stores	ACV** Share	# of Stores	ACV*** Share	# of Stores	ACV*** Share
Conventional Supermarket	22,000	$131,000	14,000	30,250	55.2%	17,000	30.0%	14,500	24.9%
Superstore	41,500	264,000	22,000	3,150	11.6	5,700	20.3	6,500	22.5
Food/Drug Combo	53,000	360,000	28,000	475	2.2	1,400	6.8	1,650	7.8
Super Combo	95,000	900,000	60,000+	10	--	95	1.0	200	2.0
Warehouse Store	40,000	200,000	14,000	920	2.5	2,900	7.8	2,400	6.3
Super Warehouse	57,500	550,000	22,000	7	--	400	3.0	525	3.8
Hypermarket	175,000	1,500,000	100,000+	--	--	18	.2	35	.5
Limited Assortment	10,000	60,000	800	750	.6	470	.4	720	.6
Wholesale Club	104,000	865,000	5,000	8	--	380	3.1	500	4.0
Convenience Store (Traditional)	2,500	11,000*	3,400	35,800	5.4	52,000	7.7	53,000	7.6
Convenience Store (Petroleum-based)	--	8,500*	--	--	--	31,000	3.5	32,500	3.6
Other	NA	18,500	NA	96,000	22.5	65,000	16.2	67,500	16.4

*Merchandise sales only (non-gas)

**ACV (All Commodity Volume) reflects adjustment for general merchandise not commonly found in other food store formats.

***Minimum $2 million in annual sales.

Source: Competitive Edge, (May 1990).

mies of scale, reduction of volatility of input prices, or assurance and consistency of supply is difficult to say.

Financial Structure. Although financial information is often considered a measure of performance, it also sets up certain goals and boundaries in an industry and, as such, can be interpreted as an index of industry competitiveness and structure. For over twenty years until 1987, Cornell University collected a wide range of confidential financial data from U.S. grocery chains and published a report that is widely regarded as the supermarket industry standard for financial information. Table 1.10 provides a five-year historical comparison of the average operating statements for the participating chains.

For the most recent five-year period, Table 1.11 shows several of the more important financial ratios from these Cornell analyses. The return on investment of grocery chains, on average, is considerably below that considered normal or even acceptable in many other related industries. While the return on net worth and the return on assets for food chains has averaged around 11 percent and 5 percent respectively, these same measures averaged approximately 22 percent and 9 percent for the soft drink industry and 20 percent and 8 percent for the tobacco industry (Salomon Brothers, 1988). Similarly, net profit (after taxes) as a percentage of sales, although rising to nearly 2.0 percent in recent years, is still far lower than, say, the comparable figure for their grocery industry manufacturing counterparts.

Table 1.12 shows three measures of return on investment for a sample of publicly held grocery chains for 1984–88. The average after-tax profits for food retailers in 1989 was 0.7 percent of sales versus 0.9 percent in 1988. This compares to an after-tax profit of 4.2 percent of sales for food processors in 1989, down from 5.5 percent in 1988. While the return on equity for food processors fell from 20.9 percent in 1988 to 16.9 percent in 1989, the same measure rose from 12.6 percent to 15.3 percent on average for all food retailers. (The range of this statistic can be seen in Table 1.10.)

NEW PRODUCTS INTRODUCTION RATE

Each year, at least for the past twenty years, the number of new products introduced into the U.S. grocery distribution system has grown. Because of the different definitions used, estimates of the precise number of new products – whether fundamentally new products or variations of existing products (e.g., new flavors or package sizes) – introduced into the grocery distribution channels range from 2,560 (Nielsen, 1987) to over 12,000 (Gorman, 1990). Gorman's *New Product Annual* defines a new product as any new product from a manufacturer, including flavors, colors or varieties but not new sizes, packages, or simple improvements.[2]

Table 1.10

Gross Margin, Expenses, and Earnings of Food Store Chains (as a percent of sales)

Item	1982-83	1983-84	1984-85	1985-86	1986-87
GROSS MARGIN	22.92	23.89	24.85	23.10	22.62
Expense					
Payroll	13.12	13.11	13.52	12.48	10.96
Supplies	1.04	0.92	1.00	0.96	0.96
Utilities	1.23	1.33	1.31	1.85	1.25
Communications	0.08	0.08	0.08	0.05	0.20
Travel	0.08	0.08	0.08	0.05	0.02
Services Purch.	1.34	1.34	1.48	0.81	0.42
Promo. Activities	0.35	0.42	0.32	0.54	0.84
Professional Services	0.08	0.09	0.07	0.55	0.46
Donations	0.01	0.01	0.02	0.04	0.08
Insurance	0.93	1.06	1.25	0.74	0.50
Taxes and licenses					
(except on income)	1.01	1.06	1.31	0.68	0.75
Property Rentals	1.43	1.43	1.45	0.76	0.76
Equipment Rentals	0.19	0.18	0.37	0.04	0.10
Depreciation & Amort.	0.89	0.94	0.72	1.17	1.10
Repairs	0.65	0.67	0.65	0.74	0.76
Unclassified	1.03	1.28	0.74	0.29	1.41
Total Exp. Before Interest	22.10	23.05	23.68	21.40	20.55
Total Interest	0.19	0.23	0.23	0.30	0.11
TOTAL EXPENSE (including interest)	22.29	23.28	23.91	21.70	20.65
NET OPERATING PROFIT	0.62	0.60	0.94	1.40	1.96
Other income or deductions					
Cash discounts earned	0.52	0.57	0.56	0.07	0.06
[1]Other revenue, net	0.25	0.36	0.17	0.33	0.36
Total Net Other Inc.	0.77	0.93	0.73	0.39	0.43
Total net earnings before income taxes	1.40	1.53	1.67	1.80	2.39
Total income taxes	0.54	0.59	0.74	0.91	0.95
Total Net Earnings after income taxes	0.86	0.94	0.93	0.89	1.45
Earnings As a % of Net Worth					
after tax earnings	9.90	9.87	10.35	12.03	15.01
Number of Stockturns	13.43	12.80	12.90	10.43	10.98
Sales (in thousand $)					
Avg. per store	8.687	9.169	9.680	9.188	7.204
Avg. per identical store	8.385	9.202	9.464	9.353	7.412
Base: Number of Chains	51	46	55	32	32

[1]Includes profit or loss on real estate.

Source: Cornell University Research Report (1987).

Table 1.11
Financial Ratios and Return on Investment for Grocery Chains

	1983-84	1984-85	1985-86	1986-87
Financial Ratios				
Current assets to liabilities	1.33	1.42	1.49	1.39
Net sales to total assets	4.83	4.78	4.69	4.41
Net sales to net worth	10.54	11.18	10.26	10.32
Net worth to total assets	0.46	0.43	0.46	0.43
Return on Investment				
Net earnings/assets (%)	4.52	4.42	5.50	6.41
Net earnings/worth (%)	9.87	10.35	12.03	15.01
Base: Number of chains	46	55	32	32

Source: Cornell University, *Operating Results of Food Chains* (Research reports, various years).

That new products are proliferating is beyond doubt: the number of introductions in 1989 was nearly three times the 1970–81 annual average. Although the growth rates differ considerably by category, nearly every individual category registered a steady growth over this period. The total number of products grew by 66 percent—from 7,271 in 1984 to 12,051 in 1989 (Gorman, 1990). Industry leaders have frequently voiced their alarm over the dimensions of new product proliferation and its implications:

"We are concerned with the big battle going on between the major manufacturers for a share of market. It requires them to get new products first . . . and these products are obviously very costly to maintain. We are looking very carefully at the situation—the tremendous expense of reslotting the warehouse, changing our shelf allocation—we are very concerned about the gross profit contribution," said Harold Greenberg, senior vice-president of Certified Supermarkets of Illinois in a recent roundtable discussion of retailers, wholesalers, and manufacturers sponsored by *Supermarket News* (1984a).

Greenberg was not the only participant to voice concern about the proliferation of new products in the food industry. With an estimated 94 percent failure rate of new products, industry officials at all levels are analyzing the implications, both good and bad, of the phenomenon dubbed "new product mania." Brooke Lennon, vice-president of merchandising, Grand Union Company, pointed out, "Almost 99.9 percent of the new items that are accepted cause another item to be discontinued." The economic implications for wholesalers and retailers are profound, and selection of new product lines at these levels is critical (*Supermarket News*, 1984b).

Table 1.12
Return on Investment for Selected Supermarket Chains, 1984–1988

Company	Return on Revenues (%)					Return on Assets (%)					Return on Equity (%)				
	1984	1985	1986	1987	1988	1984	1985	1986	1987	1988	1984	1985	1986	1987	1988
Albertson's Inc.	1.7	1.7	1.9	2.1	2.4	8.1	7.9	8.4	9.4	10.9	18.8	17.5	18.0	19.9	22.2
American Stores Co.-New	1.5	1.1	1.0	1.1	0.5	7.2	4.4	4.1	4.3	1.8	30.4	17.9	14.9	15.0	8.5
Brunos Inc.	2.6	2.8	3.0	2.7	2.2	12.8	12.4	11.5	10.5	9.6	24.5	20.7	18.3	16.4	19.0
Delchamps Inc.	1.5	1.5	1.2	0.8	1.0	7.6	7.0	5.1	4.0	5.0	17.1	15.2	11.5	9.1	12.9
Food Lion Inc. -CL A	2.5	2.6	2.6	2.9	3.0	12.3	12.3	11.8	12.2	11.9	26.0	25.7	26.2	28.4	29.2
Giant Food Inc. -CL A	2.1	2.5	1.8	2.8	3.3	8.9	9.8	6.7	9.2	10.5	21.4	22.8	16.3	23.1	25.0
Great A & P Tea Co.	0.9	0.8	0.9	1.1	1.3	4.0	3.7	3.7	4.8	5.2	10.6	9.0	9.7	12.9	14.0
Hannaford Bros. Co.	1.6	1.8	2.1	2.3	2.3	6.5	6.8	7.9	8.6	8.4	16.8	16.3	16.8	18.5	18.8
Kroger Co.	1.0	1.1	0.3	1.0	0.2	4.4	4.6	1.4	4.3	0.8	14.1	15.5	4.7	17.4	NM
Pueblo International	0.6	0.9	0.9	NM	NA	2.3	3.5	3.1	NM	NA	6.7	10.8	11.6	NM	NA
Weis Markets Inc.	5.8	5.9	5.9	6.7	6.9	15.4	14.9	14.5	15.0	14.6	18.2	17.5	16.9	17.6	17.1
Winn-Dixie Stores Inc.	1.6	1.4	1.4	1.3	1.3	10.0	9.0	9.0	8.1	8.0	19.5	17.2	17.2	15.6	15.9

Source: Standard & Poor's Compustat Services, Inc.

GATEKEEPER ROLE OF THE BUYER

The relentless stream of new products creates continuous pressure on grocery headquarters buyers – gatekeepers to the supermarket shelves – to decide quickly which new products to accept. Although not all new products are introduced to all supermarkets, maximum distribution is critical to new product success; thus, most new products are introduced to the principal integrated grocery wholesale-retail companies. Consequently, grocery company procurement staffs may evaluate as many as several hundred new products certain weeks of the year. The criteria they employ for these evaluations and their decision rules bear directly on the design of the manufacturers' new product development and marketing strategies (particularly with the vast costs at stake), the structure of the retailer evaluation system and their costs, and importantly, overall systemwide performance and consumer choice. Buyer decision processes, however, remain a relatively unstudied area. The following chapter reviews the existing literature and studies that shed some light on this area.

NOTES

1. Much of the discussion in this section draws from Marion (1986). Although the focus of this book is all grocery products, food as well as nonfood, when this section describes manufacturers, it refers primarily to food manufacturers. On the other hand, structural description of retailers includes both food and nonfood categories within the retail store.

2. Later in this book, when reporting empirical research conducted with one particular grocery company, our own classification of new products does encompass all new products – that is, all new Stock Keeping Units (SKUs) presented to the retailer, including new sizes, packages, and other improvements. We adopted this classification system since, for the retailer, each different package size, flavor, and other features requires a separate order number, scanning code, inventory slot, and sometimes price and thus can fairly be treated as a different product.

2

KEY PARTICIPANTS IN
THE NEW PRODUCT
INTRODUCTION PROCESS

SYSTEMWIDE INTEGRATIVE FRAMEWORK

Even a casual consideration of the enormous number of potential factors influencing new product introductions, from both the manufacturer and the retailer perspectives, suggests the need for some type of organizational tool to help isolate and better examine the various steps of the process. Yet ready-made tools appropriate to explain the new product behavior and strategy of participants are unavailable.

Although the management and organizational theory literature is rich in its treatment of internal firm behavior, relatively little of this work has penetrated mainstream economic analysis, and virtually none of it is easily applicable to managerial decision making. This situation is part of the general neglect by economists, agricultural economists, and other researchers alike of management strategy and conduct (behavior). To the extent that economic behavior has been studied, however, it has generally been through the work of industrial organizational (IO) economics and, specifically, work with the structure-conduct-performance (S-C-P) paradigm. D. R. Henderson and B. W. Marion, however, have noted that even IO theory rarely explicitly considers the firm decision environment, at either the manufacturer or distributor level. Furthermore, in the late 1980s, several researchers identified internal firm decision-making and strategic behavior as high-priority research areas. Thus, a number of prominent researchers have drawn attention to a critical area of study – business decision making and strategy formulation – in which comparatively little work has been done and for which few proved conceptual frameworks exist. One of our aims in this book is to contribute to the remedy of this situation.

The conceptual model guiding our analysis of the behavior of the supermarket buyer to accept or reject a new grocery product is presented in Figure 2.1, which builds on the S-C-P paradigm. The approach elaborates the often neglected conduct dimension, referred to by many researchers as a black box, of manufacturer-distributor exchanges specifically relating to new product behavior. Although few would deny that strategic behavior is critical to performance results, strategic behavior has not generally made its way into economic models in the same way that the other two dimensions of the S-C-P paradigm, structure and performance, have. Indeed, a major strain of the IO literature is known simply as structure-performance studies for this reason. F. M. Scherer (1980) suggested that conduct (used somewhat interchangeably here with *behavior* or *strategic behavior*) has not received adequate research attention for two principal reasons. First, the standard analytical tools of economists, in particular, econometric analysis, generally require precise and easily measurable variables to fit into quantifiable models. Obviously this is difficult or impossible with many behavioral variables. A second problem in the past has been the lack of researcher access to the data necessary to conduct any analysis, regardless of type. Internal firm data are generally confidential. Our

Figure 2.1
Conceptual Approach to New Product Conduct

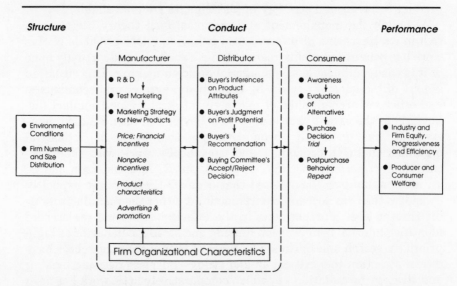

Note: Feedback loops are not shown here.

Source: E. W. McLaughlin and V. R. Rao, "The Strategic Role of Supermarket Buyer Intermediaries in New Product Selection: Implications for Systemwide Efficiency," *American Journal of Agricultural Economics* 72 (May 1990).

study has developed an approach that attempts to remedy both of these traditional constraints.

Our expanded conduct model implies that a new product's acceptance, and, ultimately, system efficiency and performance, is a function first of manufacturer and distributor structure (e.g., firm number and size distribution) and subsequently of the strategies and decision-making procedures of both sets of firms. For example, subsequent to the generation of a new product idea, a prototype is developed and modified through various phases of R&D activity and consumer research before an initial marketing strategy for the item is established by the manufacturer. Test marketing might be conducted. The new item may then be presented to the buyer-intermediary. Effectively, the buyer evaluates the new product's likely demand and profit potential (modeling of buyer's judged profit potential has been reported in McLaughlin and Rao, 1988) based on the information (e.g., marketing strategy) presented by the manufacturer. The main marketing factors typically include price and other financial incentives (e.g., margin structure, credit, forward-buy provisions), promotional factors (e.g., coupons, in-store signage), advertising campaigns, various physical aspects (e.g., taste, appearance) of the new product, and, often, certain nonprice incentives (e.g., free goods, delivery scheduling, slotting allowances).

A number of opportunities for contact and negotiation between manufacturer and distributor (used interchangeably to refer to both wholesale and retail intermediaries) occur during this process. Distributors may at times initiate the idea of developing a new item with a manufacturer based on perceived market demand; manufacturers sometimes make use of buyer judgment as a proxy for a test market or often share results of any preliminary test marketing for retailer reaction; manufacturers frequently alter certain marketing strategy variables (especially nonprice incentives) based on the suggestions made by retailers. Thus, our conceptual model depicts the critical transmittal of information vertically, externally between manufacturer and retailer (intermediary), as well as the internal decision making within each firm.

Often after repeated contacts with the supplier, the buyer makes a recommendation to a buying committee. This committee, which normally consists of senior executives who represent the firm's diverse interests, makes the final decision, nearly always in accordance with the buyer's recommendation.

The final decision by the buyer serves generally to reinforce a process that may already have been initiated by the manufacturer's promotional program: the stimulation of consumer awareness and demand. Through a wide spectrum of activities, manufacturers and retailers, often in concert, attempt to ensure that consumers are made aware of the new product and have the means to evaluate the product with both new and existing alternative offerings. Subsequently, the consumer may decide to try the product and, if satisfied, may become a repeat purchaser. Consumer satisfaction and welfare in its many forms are perhaps among the best overall indexes of the performance of any economic system.

MANUFACTURERS' ROLE

A detailed description of the roles of the participants presented in Figure 2.1 is fundamental to a more complete understanding of the new product development process. The role of the manufacturer, among the major participants in this process, has been the most thoroughly researched. Indeed, a rich literature exists that identifies and details the critical steps that manufacturers typically take in creating and bringing new products to market.[1]

Manufacturer Incentives for New Products

The 1980s brought an increased emphasis on formalized market research, marketing strategy, and decision making. As competition in the grocery industry and most other industries intensified, as consumer preferences became more fragmented, and as external social, economic, and political pressures continued to exert themselves, most companies recognized that the era of casual marketing was over. Plans for new products could no longer be developed intuitively; the cost of failure had become too great. Thus, marketing planning in general, and new product planning in particular, took on increased importance in most companies.

New products themselves have become a much more important part of manufacturers' portfolios. Chapter 1 presented data showing the dramatic rise in the number of new products in virtually all categories. Manufacturers cite many reasons to explain the explosion of new products and their elevated role in today's marketing strategies. First, many point out that new products are necessary to maintain the interest of channel intermediaries (e.g., wholesale and retail headquarters buyers) and consumers. New products are seen as the principal way to stimulate growth, cash flow, market share, and profit, the ultimate goals of most organizations. Second, some new products are launched to counter a competitor's new or expected entry. This is often felt necessary to protect hard-fought-for market and shelf space positions. Indeed, waiting to see the initial marketplace response to a competitor's new product and then, if successful, improving on it can sometimes lead to a new dominant position.

Extending an item to an adjacent product space to attract incremental business or to leverage a brand by means of a so-called line-item extension is a growing force driving new product introductions (Exhibit 2.1). New products are also introduced to reduce the costs of an existing product, to take advantage of new technologies or processes (e.g., microwave food products), to respond to changes in consumer demand (e.g., new interest in low-calorie food, fewer additives) to transform a commodity to a higher value-added item (e.g., the branding of fresh meat), and to ensure partially against high new product failure rates.

This last justification has been a powerful motivator as firms struggle to survive and succeed. Failure rates vary from 10 to 90 percent, depending on the research reported (Crawford, 1979). This vast disparity is explained by the different industries in which the rates are assessed, the various definitions of new product employed, and the time at which the offering is determined a failure. For example, should a product be considered a failure if it never becomes successfully commercialized, if it never gets into the store, if it is discontinued by the retail chain after six months (or nine or twelve months), or if it does not attain targeted sales goals? One source (Cochran and Thompson, in Hisrich and Peters, 1984, p. 15) attributed new product failures to the following problems:

Inadequate market analysis	32 percent
Product defects	23 percent
Higher costs than anticipated	14 percent
Poor timing	10 percent
Competition reaction	8 percent
Inadequate marketing effort (includes weaknesses in sales force, distribution, and advertising)	13 percent

Robert D. Buzzell and Robert E. M. Nourse (in Hisrich and Peters, 1984, p. 15) substantiate these findings by concluding that about 80 percent of the reasons given for discontinuing a new product resulted from "marketing misjudgments or inadequacies."

Frameworks in Which to Consider New Products

New product development and management have been viewed from a number of useful conceptual frameworks.

Product Life Cycle (PLC). This concept has occupied a prominent place in the marketing literature as both a guideline for managing product strategy and as a forecasting tool. Borrowing from the notion

Exhibit 2.1
What's in a Name?

A recent article in *Advertising Age* (June 17, 1990) revealed that the nation's consumer goods companies have run out of major brand names to exploit as line extensions. The 1990s, it asserts, will see the return of large-scale new product introductions. Between 1979 and 1989, the article explains, line extensions increased from 22 percent to 62 percent of all new products marketed, and some industry analysts feel that line extensions, while giving "more bang for the marketing buck at first," have a diminishing effect on the consumer, to the point where new brand names make more sense.

But line extensions are still the rage among manufacturers, and judging from the success of the products, many brand names are alive and well and giving birth to equally successful line extensions. Gender-specific diapers are a good example. Procter & Gamble launched the first product, Luvs for boys and Luvs for girls, in early 1989. Kimberly-Clark Corporation launched a line extension of Huggies Super-Trim diapers, Huggies for Him and Huggies for Her, in 1990. Gender-specific Pampers (Procter & Gamble) were also introduced in 1990, and private label diaper manufacturers are likely to follow suit soon.

Ironically, some of the first victims of the explosion in sex-specific diapers are the original diaper products themselves. Supermarket managers are faced with the dilemma of too many varieties of diapers and too little space and have decided to narrow the range of products. "To make room, you either have to expand the section or cut some sizes. We have had to cut down to carrying just a few of the different sizes. The diapers come in package sizes from twelve-count to ninety-six-count. We cannot carry every one of them in both boy and girl," says Steve Davis, grocery buyer, Sunset Foods, Highland Park, Illinois. The situation is especially critical for smaller stores. Some have stopped stocking the largest sized packages of diapers, and others have dumped the small twelve- or eighteen-count packages.

Manufacturers have responded to the diaper crunch by developing higher compression packaging and promoting shelf designs that can accommodate the different line extensions. But most drastic is the decision by P&G to phase out unisex diapers altogether. While some retailers feel that there is still a place for unisex diapers, for convenience and price, many industry analysts feel that the gender specifics are here to stay and that consumers will buy diapers just as they do any other clothing for their babies. Scott Stewart, public affairs manager for Procter & Gamble, points out that the gender-specific diapers offer tailor-made absorbency, so the diapers work better. "Esthetics, such as having pink and blue, may be the first reason to buy, but performance keeps them coming back." The well-established brand names don't hurt either.

Pasta sauces are close on the heels of diapers as successful line extensions, with an annual growth of 10 percent. A recent survey indicates that 80 percent of the category is shared by the brands of three manufacturers: Unilever (Ragu), Campbell (Prego), and Borden (Classico). Aunt Millie's and Prince brands together account for another 10 percent. All-natural, exotic, and up-scale varieties show growth, while traditional spaghetti sauce still occupies the

Exhibit 2.1 (*cont.*)

---

strongest position within the category. Such line extensions as all-natural, garden-style, and chunky versions of the old standbys are in demand.

Once again, the major problem facing retailers is the lack of space for the ever-growing variety of products. A recent article in *Supermarket News* (August 20, 1990) demonstrates the lengths to which retailers have had to go to keep up with the line extensions and the consumers' demand for them. Terry Stadheim, grocery buyer for Hughes Markets, Los Angeles, says, "We have had to redo the entire aisle of pasta, pasta sauce and boxed pasta dinners to accommodate the new items."

And when looking at the popularity and success of line extensions, one cannot forget the product dubbed "Brand of the Decade" in a January 1990 *Advertising Age* review of the 1980s: Diet Coke. This first-ever line extension of the Coke trademark was introduced in 1982 and quickly became not only the nation's leading diet soft drink but the third leading soft drink in sales, behind only regular Coke and Pepsi. While *Advertising Age* acknowledged that Diet Coke's performance on the marketing front was a key element of its phenomenal success, "clearly the Coca-Cola name strapped more horsepower to the diet brand." While one of the casualties of Diet Coke's meteoric rise was Coca-Cola's Tab diet drink, the sacrifice is well worth the (low-calorie) sweetness of success – Diet Coke is perhaps the most successful line extension ever.

---

of a biological life cycle, this concept charts the life of a product from its conception and birth, through the various stages of growth until maturity and, finally, decline (and death). Although this cycle does not hold for all products, empirical research has confirmed its validity for a wide range of consumer products (Buzzell and Nourse, 1967). The standard progression can be seen in the S curve of Figure 2.2.

The basic notion underlying the product life cycle is that firms should strive to produce a balanced portfolio of products, that is, distributed along the product life cycle curve. According to this concept, a blend of products, old and new, represents a low-risk approach to ensure continuous cash flow; more mature products generate cash surpluses to support the creation and development of new products.

The product life cycle is divided into four well-defined stages.

The *introductory stage* sales of the new product are low and grow only modestly. Consumers are either not yet aware of the product or are reluctant to buy it until it has had time to prove itself. Profits are often negative at this stage since the sales are not high enough to cover the high fixed (and sunk) costs of research and development and the high operating costs of ensuring the product a place in the distribution system. The new product manager must try to expand distribution outlets and build consumer awareness and confidence. Promotion, advertising, working with channel intermediaries (buyers at distributor headquar-

Figure 2.2
Stages of Product Life Cycle

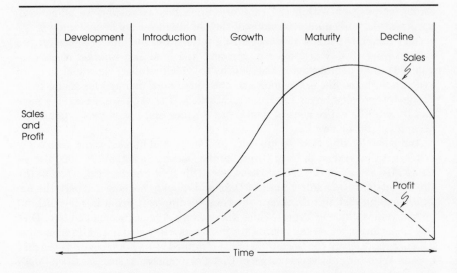

ters), and increasing production to meet anticipated demand are activities that characterize the manufacturer's role during this stage.

The *growth stage* is associated with rapid sales expansion. As advertising and promotion succeed in making more people aware of the product and the pipelines begin to fill, the management challenge shifts. Here, the marketer's task is to adjust production and the marketing mix (pricing, distribution, promotion and product attributes) in such a way as to discourage competition. If this stage is properly managed, sales should result in profits.

The *maturity stage,* where most products are found and thus where most competitive battles are staged, is reached next. Sales growth slows as markets become saturated with the product, now with numerous competition attracted by the sales and earnings growth of the previous stages, and competition intensifies. Managers often take dramatic action – creative, expensive, and defensive – during this stage to guarantee a product's prosperity and survival. New promotions or positioning, cost-cutting tactics, market expansion (including sometimes export markets), and product and packaging modifications typify this stage.

Finally, products may reach the *decline stage.* Sales drop and profits decline, according to the PLC pattern. Depending on the product, this stage may last for years, or if consumer tastes change rapidly, the product may be discontinued in a matter of months. Marketers often pursue one of two strategies during this stage. If decline of the product appears irreversible, much of the marketing support can be withdrawn in order to reduce expenses and recoup what profit may be left in the short run. This strategy, however, tends to be a self-fulfilling prophecy; without marketing support, any doubt about whether the product was in temporary or permanent decline can now be laid to rest. In the absence of promotion and advertising, further, perhaps dramatic, deterioration in performance can be expected.

Alternatively, once sales have peaked and appear poised for decline, many managers seek new uses for or adaptations to the product that may serve to extend the PLC upward and, thus, the life of the product. A classic example of this approach is given by the experience of Tide, the Procter & Gamble detergent. Although introduced in 1947, P&G has managed to avoid the PLC's prescribed decline by a relentless pursuit of product changes; at least fifty-five major improvements have been made to Tide over the last four decades. Presumably these improvements have stimulated demand for both new and repeat purchases in such a way as to circumvent the "death stage" forecast by the conventional PLC (Bagozzi, 1986, p. 150). This latter strategy to develop line extensions to existing products helps explain the large number of new product introductions discussed in the previous chapter.

Although the evidence for the length, the exact shape, and even the existence of the product life cycle is mixed, there is no doubt that at least for major categories of products, the product life cycle has been a useful conceptual framework within which managers are able to view or make decision about and project the strategy of their products.

Product Portfolio Analysis. In the 1960s the Boston Consulting Group (BCG) took the leadership in a research trend that culminated in a relationship between cost and accumulated production (volume) that became known as the experience curve. Essentially this curve documents a relationship across many industries where unit costs are observed to decline as experience and, thus, accumulated production increase because of a number of factors, such as greater labor efficiencies, more specialization of work activities, production innovations, and standardization of production techniques. The experience curve became the foundation of a related concept, the growth share matrix, also developed by the BCG.[2]

The growth share matrix, often simply called the BCG matrix, categorizes products, new and old, in terms of their cash flow. The experience curve provides an important part of the rationale for the BCG framework since it is believed that the lower costs that result from greater accumulated production (i.e., experience) will lead to greater market share, one of the essential indicators of corporate health, according to the matrix. Each quadrant of the matrix is defined by measures of the market growth rate (vertical axis) and market share position (horizontal axis). The matrix is presented in Figure 2.3. The placement of the products of a company's portfolio into quadrants of the matrix determines the types of strategic options available to management.

Products in the upper-left-hand quadrant, or "stars" in BCG terminology, have a relatively large share of the market and a high growth rate. Considerable amounts of cash are needed in order to sustain these levels of growth. Special promotions, high sales costs, lack of economy, and keen competition attracted by the twin appeal of high growth and

Figure 2.3
A Modified BCG Matrix

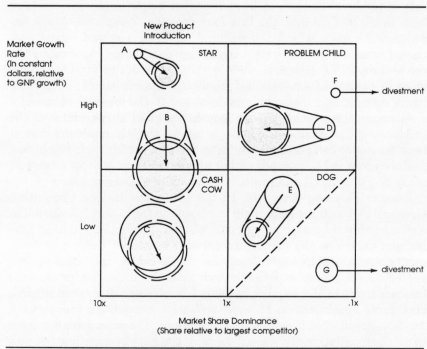

Forecast position of product   Present position

Source: Reprinted from *Journal of Marketing,* Published by the American Marketing Association, Chicago, IL 60606. George S. Day, "Diagnosing the Product Portfolio," August 1977.

few market leaders force the firm with a star to lavish great sums of cash to maintain and strengthen its position.

Products in the upper-right quadrant are referred to as "problem children" or "question marks" since the prescription is less clear. These are products located in a category enjoying rapid growth but for which the firm's own entry has a relatively small share of the market. These products may formerly have been stars or even cash cows that had their positions eroded. Management must make a decision here as to how and whether these products can be maneuvered back toward a higher share of the market. As the arrows indicate, two strategic prescriptions are possible when a firm is confronted with a question mark business unit: divest (business F) or invest in the unit (business D) to increase its market share and move it leftward toward the star quadrant.

In the lower-right quadrant of Figure 2.3, the so-called dogs are found. As the name implies, these are products with low sales dominance that are experiencing slow growth. The manager of a dog is frequently faced with the dilemma of a product with unlikely growth possibilities and thus must make a decision regarding whether to divest the business. This is a complex decision that has implications for other, perhaps complementary, products in the business's line of products. Sometimes less drastic measures might be taken – cost cutting or minor product repositioning – that may redress the situation short of total abandonment of the product.

Finally, Figure 2.3 shows the cash cow type of product. These are often products that have reached maturity in a product life cycle and experience curve sense and have descended from star category. Since the market is no longer growing at a rapid enough rate to require the constant reinvestment required in the star category, management can now devote attention to managing a business with a dominant market share and a large cash flow. These cash stocks can then be used to support products elsewhere in the matrix that need infusions of cash to compete. Stars need further product and distribution development, and question marks often need repositioning.

After considering their products in this way, managers at company headquarters may use the BCG matrix as a framework to determine long-run investment strategy and growth directions for the current portfolio of products and may be able to identify unoccupied marketplace niches and thus new product opportunities. When used effectively, the BCG matrix provides managers with insight necessary to balance the current and future mix of products to optimize cash flow and to meet company objectives.[3]

Perceptual Positioning. In developing strategic plans for new products, perceptual maps are often used. This is typically a graphic representation with the product located on a figure in two dimensions generally selected to capture the essential attributes of the product as perceived by the target group of customers or consumers. The perceptual map, similar to the BCG matrix analysis, serves important functions. It permits management to situate its products visually in relation to competing products in terms of the key dimensions of the products. Thus, strengths and weaknesses in position can be more easily determined, and management can identify opportunities for new products or perhaps gain insights in necessary modifications to existing products in order to strengthen their competitive position regarding other products occupying the same perceptual space.

A hypothetical perceptual map of the beer market in northern California is presented in Figure 2.4. The two dimensions selected to describe the available beers are heavy/light and bitter/mild. Then, either by asking for the perceptions of one or many consumers, the various beers are located in the quadrants defined by the two dimensions. Since the brands cover much of the map, one may conclude that consumers believe that beers differ to a considerable degree along these two dimensions. From this map, management can identify its closest competitors, the most important attributes for its product, at least for the given sample of consumers, and, importantly, untapped or underutilized potential. It appears, for example, that no beer currently exists that is perceived of as light and bitter. Depending on the number of people who actually have a preference for such a beer, this may represent an opportunity for the beer manufacturer.

Organizing for New Products

Manufacturers' decisions regarding new products are among the most strategic that they face; risk, failure, and costs are high. Moreover, the mix of products in a firm's portfolio plays a crucial role in determining the types of employees and technical staff, in shaping the corporate culture, and in defining and positioning the whole organization. Because of these factors, attention to the optimal organization for new products is essential. Responsibility for the various activities required in both development and marketing of new products must be explicitly defined.[4]

Firm size is an important determinant of the way in which new product activity is organized. Perhaps it goes without saying that the smaller the firm is, the greater is the likelihood that a few people will be responsible for new product planning. Often in the smallest firms, the extreme case being the entrepreneurial firm, new product planning is vested in top management, perhaps even the chief executive officer (CEO). One or more members of the top management team will be responsible for generating new product ideas, for screening, and for de-

termining their ultimate feasibility. These decisions are predicated on
company goals and objectives and company capability to produce and
market the product. In the small firm, the CEO or president may actually supervise or carry out these functions personally. In large firms,
this is rarely possible. A number of different organizational types are
available for large firm adaptation. (These alternatives also offer insight useful for small firm managers in formalizing and professionaliz-
ing their own firm's new product efforts.) For large organizations, the
alternative organizational structures for new product development
generally can be categorized into one of four types.

New Product Department. Sometimes also called product planning
or market development department, this structure attempts to central-
ize the new product decision-making process and avoid the redundancy
of tasks across divisions of a company. Generally the director of such a
department is a senior executive, often reporting directly to the president or executive vice-president. Although some firms choose to place
new product department as a staff and others as a line function, the
essential challenge is to ensure that the lines of communication and
authority are clear and that internal political posturing does not inter-

Figure 2.4
One Beer Drinker's Perceptual Map of the Beer Market in Northern California

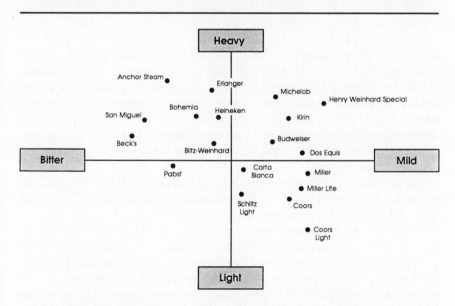

Source: Reprinted with permission of Macmillan Publishing Company from *Principles of
Marketing Management* by Richard P. Bagozzi. Copyright © Science Research
Associates, Inc., 1986.

fere with the efficiency and performance of the department. Most often, a new product department oversees the following functions: suggesting new product objectives, examining new ideas, assisting in developing new product specifications, implementing test marketing, and coordinating all interdepartmental effort during the new product process.

Manufacturer New Product Committee. Some organizations prefer that new product decisions be made by individuals from a variety of departments. These individuals are charged with certain new product responsibilities for a portion of their time but generally are more occupied with their normal obligations and activities as managers or staff in other departments. Although overall the functions to be performed for a new product – idea generation, screening, and so forth – do not change, the committee structure generally organizes these functions much less systematically than in a formalized new product department. Although this lack of a rigorous systematic approach has its weakness – such as an arguably inefficient use of top management time and an unavoidable fragmented approach to the new product evolution – it is probably the most often used structure for new product planning because of its inherent flexibility. In addition, committee structures have the advantage that they can pool expertise from disparate areas, have to meet only when needed, and are generally composed of senior managers so their ideas can often be implemented quickly.

Product Manager. Procter & Gamble introduced the product, or brand, manager concept in 1931. Although its interpretation and responsibilities have continued to change – now, Procter & Gamble brand managers report to thirty-six category managers to allow for a better coordination with trade buyer organizations – the product manager today in many firms retains the responsibility of high-level planning and decision making for a product or group of products. Ideally each product manager is furnished with all the resources required to manage the product totally. However, product managers are also generally looked to for leadership in developing new products, particularly when a line extension is being considered. Thus, product managers can be expected to assist in the coordination of nearly all aspects of new product planning, from brainstorming ideas to engineering design, to market testing and budgeting. The one serious limitation often cited when discussing the many benefits of product management is that too often the product manager's authority is frequently not consistent with his or her responsibilities. He or she often may have to resort to personality or charisma to get tasks accomplished within the company since formal lines of authority may not exist.

Venture Team. When new products do not fit exactly with historical or current operations of a business, a venture team may be established. Composed of individuals from a variety of functional areas, it generally remains somewhat apart from the rest of the organization, enjoys a certain independence and freedom from time pressures, and often reports to the CEO directly. This is usually the least permanent of all the organizational structures, but because of the proximity, top management is able to exert considerable influence on final decisions.

New Product Budgeting

The amount of money required to develop a new product is a function of a combination of corporate, market, and environmental conditions. Corporate objectives and capabilities, as well as competitive activities, will play a role, especially in initial budget setting. However, after a consideration of the range of alternatives circumscribed by these constraints, budget allocation normally follows standard corporate procedures for capital investment decisions, although special guidelines or rules of thumb are often employed for new products.

Average expenditures for new product development by the industry as a whole or by the firm's direct competitors often serves as an initial basis. However, since the competitive data needed to make these comparison are often not accessible and because they are not publicly available, research and development (R&D) numbers are imperfect proxies, and setting new product budgets remains imprecise. To some extent this uncertainty can be dealt with by the application of Bayesian decision theory.[5]

New Product Planning and Development

Product planning and development proceeds as a function of firm size, strategic orientation, and technological requirements. Generally, however, it follows the patterns indicated in Figure 2.5 and can be divided into five distinct stages: idea stage, concept stage, product development stage, test marketing stage, and commercialization.

The generation of a large number of innovative ideas is essential at the outset of the planning process, since after intense internal screening and test marketing, very few ideas will survive. This is particularly true if performance and valuative criteria are to be kept strict in order to avoid introducing an inferior product. There exists a long list of creative problem-solving techniques that are frequently employed to stimulate the generation of product ideas. They range from comparatively well-known and straightforward approaches such as brainstorming and checklists to more arcane and scientific methods such as bisociative thinking and synectics (Hisrich and Peters, 1984, p. 132ff.). Each of the

Figure 2.5
The Product Planning and Development Process

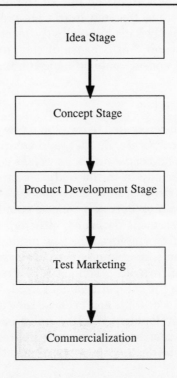

ideas ultimately generated should be carefully evaluated to determine which, if any, are promising.

Ideas that pass initial screening enter the concept stage, where the idea is developed more thoroughly. Generally initial business plans and marketing programs are put together during this stage. The target market is defined, and several potential buyers and users of the potential product are contacted for their reaction to the concept. If the team responsible for the concept evaluation decides that the product is technically feasible, is consistent with overall corporate objectives, has an appropriately sized expected demand, and is likely to generate profits in accord with corporate expectations, the concept is approved.

Next, a prototype is developed. At this, the product development stage, the product receives vigorous internal technical testing, often in laboratory conditions, and is pilot tested with production teams and reevaluated by internal consumer panels. If an actual test market is employed as a last stage before introduction and full-scale commercialization, consumer response is gauged.

Test marketing, the next stage, has become very costly. An outlay of $1 million for a 3 to 5 percent U.S. test market was the norm in 1989 (Gorman, 1989, p. 18). As a result, it is being used less frequently than was the practice for new products ten years ago. Before undertaking a test market, a number of key factors must be analyzed. First, the costs of failure have to be evaluated against the potential rewards of success. If the costs of failure are low, often the test market is dispensed with, and the product is passed on immediately to the commercialization stage. Moreover, the additional time that the competition has to assess the product during the test market period and perhaps develop its own version of the product must be evaluated against the potential benefits of the test. Some marketing analysts use the Bayesian approach of an expected-value decision rule to determine whether to test market the product. Typically the product is tested if the expected monetary value of all states of nature associated with testing the product is greater than the costs of the test market.

After a positive determination is made regarding whether to undertake a test market, all efforts must be made to avoid distorting the results of the test. The objective of the test is to give as accurate a picture of the marketplace conditions as possible so as to use the results of the test to make last-minute modifications to the product, the package, the positioning, and the forecasted sales estimate. Site selection, for example, is critical; markets should be considered only if they mirror the norms of the ultimate target market. If this product is ultimately to be sold in national markets, then the characteristics of the consumers, the competition, the media mix, and the distribution system should parallel those of the national market. Furthermore, in order to represent the ultimate intended market target as accurately as possible, the size of the test market must be adequate. Several statistical frameworks are available to assist with the determination of sample size (see, for example, Hisrich and Peters, 1984, p. 220). The design of the test itself, a crucial dimension, will be determined by the product and the marketing plan.

Because of the increasingly high costs of test marketing and the often questionable nature of their results, a number of alternatives are available. Consumer panels, for example, can be used to gauge consumers' likely reaction, especially in the short term, to the new product. Market chain analysis can be employed to give marketers insight into the dynamics of competition and the forces influencing consumers to engage in brand switching. One technique that is growing in sophistication and, resultingly, usage as well, is computer simulation of a marketplace. Here, if the model is selected carefully, the variables that are likely to influence the success of the product in the marketplace are included in the model and produce estimates of the probable performance of the product once commercialized. Obviously, these simulations are only as good as the models and the variables that generate them. Again, a variety of different commercial models are available for the purpose of simulating test market conditions.

Throughout the course of the product planning and development process, the formulation of marketing strategies and programs should be continuous. The design of a new product marketing program involves the entire range of marketing decisions, including both short-term and long-term marketing plans. The plan should be as comprehensive as possible and include, at a minimum, the following elements: objectives, timing, budgets, forecasts, target market characteristics and positioning, and a complete description of the marketing mix variables (pricing, promotion, product, and distribution). In addition, background information, the firm's past experience, competitive activity, and alternative strategies are often included in new product marketing plans.

Each of the components in the marketing plan is linked with one another. Figure 2.6 shows how the many sources of information are combined to create and influence the determination of a new product pricing policy. As the figure amply demonstrates, the price of a new product cannot be arrived at in a vacuum. It must be determined in full view of its impact on the firm's entire price structure and policy, on the intended distribution system, on the likely price sensitivity of consumers, on packaging and branding considerations and promotional intentions, and on intended positioning in relation to the competition. In short, once the manufacturer has developed a new product idea, the challenge of marketing it follows directly. The two are interwoven. The entire new product development and marketing plan must lend itself to an adaptive experimentation philosophy and must be consistent with corporate objectives.

DISTRIBUTOR'S ROLE

The location in the grocery distribution system where manufacturers most often have the opportunity to present and discuss their new products with the retail trade is across the desk of the trade (supermarket) buyer. It is these distributors, or channel intermediaries, who make the decision on behalf of their respective grocery organizations regarding the acceptance or rejection of new products. The internal organization of trade buyers differs by company, but two principal forms are dominant: individual buyers, who essentially make all decisions themselves, and buying committees. In the buying committee format, individual buyers meet first with suppliers who are presenting new products and subsequently with committees from their own companies, who oversee

Figure 2.6
Pricing Model for a New Product

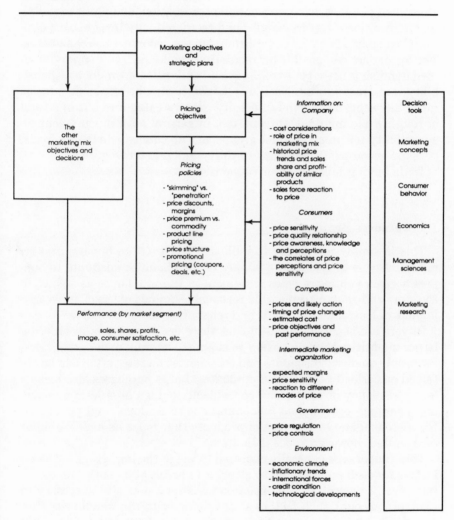

the process and effectively serve as a second screen through which the new product candidate must pass (Leed and German, 1985, p. 198).

In the past, many trade buyers also had responsibility for in-store merchandising in addition to buying duties; however, there appears to be a trend away from this dual responsibility in many distribution companies. Today, former buyer-merchandiser positions are being augmented to include new product decisions, planograms (e.g., organizing store shelf plans), pricing, promotion coordination, and profit responsibility. Traditional buyers bought and reordered only (*Progressive Grocer*, November 1989). In some firms, buyers report to merchandisers. The former are responsible for reordering, while the latter supervise all merchandising activity: working with vendors, new product responsibility, and gross profits. Each merchandiser may be responsible for as many as twenty individual direct dry grocery categories out of a total of roughly one hundred. Buyers, too, in general have procurement responsibility for broad product groups, say all canned and frozen foods, perhaps encompassing twenty to thirty individual categories.

Trade buying falls into four categories.

1. Turnover Buying

This is simply reordering to replenish stock. Often buyers' first responsibility is to maintain a supply of merchandise adequate to support a given volume of sales movement in the warehouse as well as in the store and also to keep within reasonable bounds of the charges arising out of loss, damage, theft, and rehandling of merchandise.

Buyers are generally mindful that there are advantages in ordering larger quantities than necessary to support a minimum period of sales. Favorable quantity discounts and transportation rates often can be obtained on carload or truckload purchases. Large purchases also mean a lower frequency of orders and consequent savings in ordering, receiving, handling (provided no rehandling has to be done), and paying for the merchandise. In the case of products that must be kept frozen or refrigerated, however, space is limited.

Thus, buyers are generally expected to weigh the importance of these factors for each product and to attempt to arrive at an optimum inventory level. In selecting the optimum inventory, it is also necessary to take into account such factors as the distance to the warehouse, storage requirements, and possible changes in consumer demand.

Merchandise in this turnover-buying category ordinarily is purchased on a weekly basis, and buyers endeavor to maintain a minimum supply—say at least ten days—in the warehouse. Many buyers have authority to purchase up to but not more than thirty days' supply in order to take advantage of an expected price increase.

2. Long-term Commitment Buying

Buyers for this category must ensure a continuity of supply of seasonally packed merchandise and must purchase merchandise at the current market price.

Management is often concerned about maintaining the continuity of supply of its private label merchandise. Consequently most long-term commitments a company makes are with independent packers for the supply of private label merchandise. Occasionally, when a short pack, a reduced production of a processed product, or a price increase is expected, long-term commitments are also made with national brand packers. Generally, however, nationally branded merchandise is purchased on a turnover basis.

Merchandise that is packed seasonally has to be obtained in sufficient quantities to last throughout the year, but because the price of the following year's pack might be lower, care has to be taken not to overbuy and thus end the year with a large surplus of merchandise. Usually a surplus of up to 10 percent of the annual sales volume of a product is considered normal. In estimating the probable sales of a seasonally-packed product, overall company growth, including that ascribable to new stores, is generally considered.

For a given commodity, the original estimate of annual sales is often based on the price prevailing in the current period. If the price has recently increased or is about to increase, the factor of product substitution makes it likely that less of that commodity will be sold. Consequently, the original commitment, made on a subject-to-approval-of-price basis, might have to be reduced. After the opening price is established, companies make firm commitments subject to the price at date of shipment. In the case of most long-term commitments, there is usually provision for periodic reviews during which the quantity of merchandise actually to be purchased could be adjusted.

Most buyers like to work with packers large enough to give the company a degree of operating flexibility. Nevertheless, buyers endeavor to be fair in dealing with suppliers in order to maintain good relations with them. As a result, in the event of a short pack, the distributor is usually able to procure an adequate supply of merchandise.

A large majority of long-term commitments are made between May and October, and in that period the management follows the market closely. The buyers make the initial purchasing arrangements with the packers, but final contract approval rests with the grocery sales manager, who reviews the preliminary negotiations in the light of overall company expectations and resources.

3. Special Promotion Buying

With respect to this merchandise, buyers have to decide whether special price promotions will produce great enough incremental sales to result in increased profit, notwithstanding the reduced selling price and the additional expenses of promotion. They have to keep in mind also that most retailers are constantly endeavoring to attract new customers. In some instances, therefore, merchandise that does not yield extra profit is purchased and promoted in order to strengthen the company's reputation for attractive prices. A buyer contemplating a special promotion typically confers with the grocery sales manager.

4. Buying of New Products

A product is classified as new if it is not currently handled by the company, regardless of whether competition carries it – in other words, anything that requires additional shelf space.

In many companies, decisions on new products are made informally. But when growth leads to the addition of several grocery buyers, often a formal buying committee is formed. The regular members of this committee are the head buyer, merchandise buyer, and all grocery buyers. In addition, grocery field staff (assistant zone managers) often attend the buying committee meetings on a rotating basis. They are consulted primarily on store operating problems that might arise from the addition of new merchandise. On occasion, they are also consulted on whether to purchase a particular product. In some firms, the director of consumer affairs may also be a member of the buying committee to represent consumer interests.

WHOLESALE-RETAIL BUYING COMMITTEE

In many firms, a buying committee is employed. In some firms, this committee may be more accurately described as a merchandising committee because it not only decides what products to buy or to discontinue but also determines promotional plans for the company. The committee meets generally weekly, but about half of the committees meet less often (Table 2.1). Some companies, for example, dispense with a weekly meeting if the items to be discussed consist primarily of line-item extensions and not truly new products. Normally, at the meeting, each buyer presents what he or she believes to be the most promising of

Table 2.1
Frequency of Buying Committee Meetings

Per Year	Chain Buyers	Wholesaler Buyers
1 to 25 times	15%	13%
26 times	4	9
27 to 51 times	33	33
Once a week or more	48	45
Average	43.4	42.4
Median	50	48

Source: Progressive Grocer (November 1987).

the items shown to him or her since the last meeting. "New item offer" sheets and samples of the products are generally made available at this time. In only 13 percent of retail companies can a manufacturer representative present new items directly to the buying committee (*Progressive Grocer,* November 1987).

In selecting new merchandise, buying committees often make a rough estimate of the likely sales and profits of each item. They consider many factors: the utility of the product, the type of product, what it will do for the customer, and how important or advantageous its special features are to the consumer. They try to consider the quality and value offered in relation to the price to be charged. Typically they review the advertising and promotional support available for the item and consider the strength of consumer demand that might be created. Then they explore whether competitors will carry the item, the degree of product substitution that is likely to exist, and the probable effect (opportunity cost) on the company's stores if they do not accept the item. Their estimation of gross profit involves a comparison of markup and probable movement of the particular item being considered with the markup and rate of sale of other brands or similar products.

Many senior retailing executives believe that the organizational form of the buying committee is most effective for several reasons:

1. The buying decision is not made in a charged emotional atmosphere conditioned by the personal likes and dislikes of the individual buyer; hence the product receives a more unbiased consideration through a buying committee.

2. The method utilizes the collective knowledge and experience of all buying personnel. This is increasingly important as new food products today compete for shelf space not only with other foods but with general merchandise and health and beauty aids. Achieving the optimal balance in the total product often involves accepting products in one category but deleting products in a different one. Similarly, when an item is discontinued, it comes from the same manufacturer presenting a new item only about one-third of the time (*Progressive Grocer*, November 1987).

3. The committee work provides for the orderly continuity of the buying operation through effective buyer development.

4. Participation in the committee discussion helps field personnel to gain a better understanding of the buying operation and the problems faced by chain headquarters and gives them a voice in the merchandising decisions of the company.

5. Buyers periodically review their product lines for items that should be discontinued and make specific recommendations to the committee. On occasion the grocery sales manager, or head buyer, also suggests that particular items be discontinued. Nevertheless, the final decision on discontinuing a product usually rests with the buying committee. The principal reason often given for discontinuing products is unsatisfactory action on the part of the manufacturer. In some instances, a company anticipates the effect that the introduction of a new item is likely to have on sales of an existing one and discontinues the existing item before sales decline.

Although, in general, this description of supermarket buying applies to both chain and wholesaler-independent organizations, the latter firm structure experiences a unique set of concerns. Independent store operations, for example, complain that they face all the in-store logistical problems created by new items, but because they have no warehouse, they do not get access to all the supplier inducements that their chain counterparts do. They claim that wholesale buyers do not pass along all the new product compensation fees paid them, either in the form of reduced prices or in additional promotional assistance. In a 1987 survey of independent store managers conducted by *Progressive Grocer* (December 1987), the following difficulties were reported regarding new products:

- Communications and operational problems, between suppliers and retailers or between wholesalers and retailers, that cause new products to reach store level after the suppliers' major media support has ended.

- Obtaining adequate support from vendors and their own store personnel to ensure new product success.

- General lack of follow-up evaluations by suppliers at store level when the store is independent, including lack of product information and inability to reorder new merchandise at introductory prices.

STANDARD OPERATING PROCEDURES FOR SUPERMARKET BUYERS

Numerous valuable insights are gained into the standard procurement practices of supermarket buyers from a 1987 *Progressive Grocer* study (November–December, 1987). Despite the recent explosion in the numbers of new products, the *Progressive Grocer* study demonstrates that buyers spend only a small fraction of their time on new product presentations – on average, chain buyers listen to 11.7 presentations per week (Table 2.2), each lasting approximately 20 minutes. In fact, many buyers schedule all new product presentations during one morning of the week. On the other hand, with an increasing number of reports provided by vendors and also generated internally by retailers, buyers today spend much more of their time in analyzing the new product candidate and the performance of its category and gauging its sales and profit potential. Exhibit 2.2 discusses several industry views regarding who should attend the new product presentations.

Table 2.3 sheds light on the wide range of activities engaged in by buyers at chain headquarters. A chain buyer sets the retail price for the store outlets 95 percent of the time, allowing this decision to be made at the store level in only 5 percent of the cases. The same general headquarters dominance holds true for authorizing initial distribution and

Table 2.2
Number of New Product Presentations Made to Retail Trade Buyers per Week

Per Year	Chain Buyers	Wholesaler Buyers
5 or less	40%	43%
6–10	25	32
11–15	17	14
16–20	9	6
21 or more	9	5
Average	11.7	9.1

Source: Ibid.

Exhibit 2.2
Who Attends the New Product Presentations?

Some 25 percent of retailers and 40 percent of wholesalers are presented each week with three to five pitches introducing a new product line. In a high-pressure industry where time is of the essence, who attends these meetings? Manufacturers should know who their new product presentation is aimed at and how the retailers and wholesalers delegate this important responsibility, a major point raised at a recent roundtable discussion of various supermarket industry personnel held in New York and Chicago (1981) and sponsored by *Supermarket News.*

Thomas Lowe, vice-president of merchandising, Price Chopper Supermarkets, pointed out that in his organization, "It is up to the manufacturer to make the decision as to who they feel should attend." Brooke Lennon, vice-president of merchandising, Grand Union Company, concurred and pointed out that they make every effort to get the audience the manufacturer requests, at both regional offices and the main headquarters of the company.

While manufacturers have voiced concern that the absence of key decision makers at the retail level has, on occasion, held up important discussions, the retailers pointed out that new product introduction is a major aspect of their business and is never treated by them as a routine matter to be decided without considerable input from high-level officials.

Robert Ingram, vice-president of merchandising, Roger Williams Foods Incorporated, affirmed that there is a responsibility on both sides. Retailers, he said, want to ensure that the vital personnel are available at all new product introductions, and he reminded the manufacturers to schedule ample time for the retailers to convene their key players.

Lawrence Chapman, manager, sales planning, grocery sales division, Nestle Company Incorporated, agreed with the other panel participants but also pointed out the need to get the active participation of the field sales force, at a very early stage, in order to keep one step ahead of the retailers. Both sides in the ongoing discussion of new product introduction stressed that the process must be a two-way street and that the communication between the different sectors of the industry is the best tool available to all of them.

---

discontinuing items in chain organizations. Wholesalers, however, who must give considerably more flexibility and decision-making autonomy to their independent owner-operators, give far more of the decision control to store-level managers.

Although the *Progressive Grocer* study reports that, on average, buyers turn down about 65 percent of all products presented to them, that still leaves them with the task, at least in the short run, of finding places for the remaining 35 percent of all the products offered. As the number of products, or more precisely, separate stock-keeping units (SKUs), in the average chain store approaches 18,000, the number of products is growing at a rate faster than the expanding supermarket

Table 2.3
**Decision Responsibility for Managing New Products: Headquarters Decision/
Store Level Decision**

	Chain	Wholesaler
	Percent	
Set retail price	95/5	69/31
Authorize initial distribution	90/10	43/57
Discontinue item	82/18	41/59
Use of special display	65/35	25/75
Determine location in store	74/26	33/67
Determine shelf position	66/34	29/71
Determine number of facings	59/41	28/72
Re-order new items	21/79	7/93

Source: Ibid.

(FMI, 1989). There is not enough space. Some retail companies (approximately 48 percent) have responded to this space crunch by declaring a policy of deleting one (or more) items for each one they take in. But according to results of the *Progressive Grocer* study, these companies must be in the minority since, overall, product numbers continue to grow.

Both chains and wholesalers accepted more products into their total line than they discontinued in 1987 according to the *Progressive Grocer* study, but the numbers presented in Table 2.4, including net additions, appear low. If chain buyers accept 35 percent of an average number of new product presentations of over 2,500 per year, as is reported in the *Progressive Grocer* study, the total additions to the product line should be at least twice as great as the 421 presented in Table 2.4. Probably the *Progressive Grocer* study is influenced by many small firm respondents, who are not as buffeted by new products as their larger counterparts.

CHANNEL CONTROL

Industry observers and academic researchers have discussed and written extensively about what many regard as a shift in the control of the grocery distribution channel (Bucklin and Schmalensee, 1987; Gor-

Table 2.4
Additions and Deletions of Products for a Sample of Chain and Wholesale/
Independent Companies

	Chain	Wholesale/Independents
Additions	421	323
Deletions	318	189
Total SKUs[1]	17,804	13,999

[1]Stock-keeping units.

Source: Ibid.

man Publication, 1989; *Progressive Grocer,* December 1987). Many believe that the locus of power in the channel has moved in favor of retail
firms at the expense of manufacturers. Robert Schmitz (Bucklin and
Schmalensee, 1987) offers a number of reasons for this shift. On the
manufacturer's side, he cites the lack of significant product differentiation, the decline of mass marketing, the erosion of television effectiveness, the trend toward a financial focus in lieu of a marketing focus,
manufacturer concentration and consolidation, an orientation toward
short-term promotion, and a decline in brand loyalty. To this already
formidable list, he adds the forces shaping the nonpolitical order of the
channel from retailers' perspective: a rise of retailers' own local marketing and the related growth of localized media, development of indige-
nous marketing capability, increasing retailer concentration and
consolidation, more effective use of suppliers' promotional money, more
financial clout, greater distribution efficiency, and greater availability
of information generated from retailers' own electronic technology. Finally, the strength of retailers' private label programs and their new
emphasis on perishable foods merchandising have decreased their reli-
ance on traditional packaged merchandise from national brand manufacturers.

As a consequence of these many environmental changes, retailers appear to have increased their leverage over manufacturers in the buyer-
seller negotiation: they are demanding and getting greater concessions.
Many retailers now insist that suppliers deliver smaller orders but
more frequently; they increasingly require that suppliers use their own
sales representatives to set up in-store promotional displays; some
companies fine suppliers for late or incomplete deliveries; and the majority of retailers now routinely expect the manufacturer to provide

regular, sophisticated category reports and research studies. Perhaps nowhere else is the new retailer advantage seen so clearly as in the development of the terms surrounding new product introductions.

Aware of their growing power, retailers are increasingly dictating the forms of new product introductions. Many now pressure manufacturers to buy back unsold inventory, and their demands have been a principal factor leading to the significant shift of supplier spending away from national advertising to local promotional spending (*New York Times*, October 3, 1989). In 1977 manufacturers allocated 58 percent of their marketing budgets to promotion and 42 percent to advertising; by 1987 65 percent was allocated to promotion and 35 percent to advertising (*Marketing Communication*, 1988). This shift is likely to be harmful to many manufacturers since advertising tends to build brand image and consumer loyalty in the long run, while promotional spending is much more short term oriented. In fact, promotion, in an effort to achieve large sales increases during a short period, may produce a heightened consumer sensitivity to price and result in an erosion of brand strength.

A controversial new set of features now demanded routinely by many, probably most, retailers may be referred to as channel development funds, a term that covers an array of inducements designed to assist the retailer in selling the new product and to cover the retailer costs associated with adding the product. These inducements may take the form of off-invoice price reduction, guaranteed gross margins, bill-back provisions, free goods, return privileges, and various types of slotting allowances. The controversy surrounding this last category, slotting allowances, is straightforward to explain but difficult to resolve. Essentially, retailers point out that the process of introducing new products into their warehouses and stores is a time-consuming and thus costly process. For example, retail firms incur considerable costs for the evaluation of as many as several hundred new products each week (Hamm, 1981). Further, the entry and maintenance of new data are costly in terms of personnel time and computer storage space. Each new item also involves costs for inventory control and handling, separate warehouse slots and codes, specialized retail shelf space requirements, and production of shelf signs and price tags, though estimates of the high costs of evaluation are not available. One California chain reported that new product activity absorbed approximately 2,132 hours of labor per store (*Progressive Grocer*, December 1987, p. 27). Another chain with about 100 stores reported that it spent $20 million in 1989 to add new items (*Progressive Grocer*, February 1990, p. 48). These figures cover the costs of warehousing, transporting, stocking, alerting scanning files, and merchandising the new products.

Consequently, in the early 1980s, retailers began requesting that so-called slotting fees accompany any accepted new product. These fees were to compensate retailers for the costs they bore in adding the new product to their warehouse slots and, by extension, their stores. *Slotting fees* has since become a generic term that refers to the charges to the supplier designed to cover a wide range of retailer new product costs of the type discussed. Suppliers do not deny that these costs exist, and many, perhaps most, agree that they have an appropriate role to play in absorbing some of the costs. The controversy that has embroiled much of the industry involves the level of the costs. While many retailers feel that slotting allowances often cover only about two-thirds of their new product addition costs (*Progressive Grocer,* February 1990, p. 48), most suppliers contend that retailers have effectively made slotting allowances into their own profit centers, charging suppliers far more than the actual costs incurred.

Retailers in the northeastern United States, for example, have acknowledged asking for slotting allowances ranging from $15,000 to as much as $40,000 per item, in addition to the more traditional promotional and cooperative advertising funds (*Progressive Grocer,* December 1987, p. 26). Another retailer was reported to have requested $300,000 to accept a twenty-item line into his organization (*Progressive Grocer,* February 1990, p. 43). Moreover, other fees have recently emerged. In 1989, a few retailers began charging "pay-to-stay fees" to ensure a product continued "rights" to retail shelf space. Several others instituted "failure fees": a stipulation that if a product does not meet previously agreed-upon sales and movement goals, the item will not only be discontinued at the vendor's expense, but additionally, the vendor will remit money to the wholesaler to cover miscellaneous operating costs. One wholesaler, for example, now routinely charges $2,000 per SKU for new items that do not achieve agreed-upon sales goals within ninety days (*Progressive Grocer,* February 1990, p. 43). Others have followed suit.

Exhibits 2.3 and 2.4 present industry evidence on the extent of this situation. These exhibits are the actual notification forms and letters employed by a major grocery wholesale organization to its vendors regarding its policy on the "vigorous pursuit of slotting allowances" and its initiation of the so-called failure fee. Although all the activities addressed in the exhibits shift costs directly to suppliers, the wholesaler policy emphasizes that its intent is "to share the costs of distributing [new] items in a more equitable way."

Many manufacturers are also offering more generous payment terms to wholesalers and retailers that agree to take on new products. Standard terms typically provide a 2 percent discount if the invoice is paid within ten days, or the net amount in thirty days; extending the 2 percent discount for twenty or thirty days and postponing the net due until sixty days for new products are now commonplace manufacturer pricing inducements.

Exhibit 2.3
Notification to Vendors of Retailer's Policy on Slotting Allowance and Failure Fees, 1989

Dear [*name of retailer*]:

During the past five (5) years our active item count has grown at an annualized rate of 50%. During that same time frame our cost of distributing and maintaining those new items has continued to rise. As a Retail Support Company we make every attempt to satisfy the needs of our customers by accepting new items as quickly as our system allows. However, we are at a juncture where we must communicate our concerns and our policy for accepting and maintaining items.

While we accept the premise that new items contribute to the growth of our business, we also recognize that 90% of all new items fail within the first year. This places an arduous and unacceptable burden on us and our Retailers.

Henceforth, the following policy will be adopted and adhered to by the merchandising staff at [*name of retailer*].

1. Slotting allowances will continue to be vigorously pursued on all new items.
2. A failure fee will be imposed on those items that fail to reach a mutually agreed upon sales level, ninety (90) days after the item has been placed in distribution.
3. 2%/60-day extended dating (or a cash equivalent) will be required for all new items.
4. Items that fail to reach a satisfactory sales level but are maintained due to their uniqueness in a family group will be imposed with 2%/60-day dating (or a cash equivalent) on all subsequent invoices.

This policy is effective April 1, 1989.

As always the negotiations on new items and the maintenance of slow sellers will be handled by the respective buyers. You have a right to insist that your performance requirements are met as well. It is not our intent to increase the cost of distributing items but rather to share the cost in a more equitable fashion. We aim to develop and maintain a mutually beneficial partnership so as to provide growth for all parties without placing an undue hardship on either partner.

If you have any questions or concerns, please feel free to contact me.

Sincerely,

Director of Merchandising

Exhibit 2.4
Discontinuation Policy of Retailer for Failed New Products

To Vendor:

After the 90 days if the minimum case movement/week is not achieved then the following shall result:

1. Vendor will remit to [*name of retailer*] a $2,000.00 failure fee per SKU which may be deducted from the vendor's next payment. This will cover expenses that [*name of retailer*] has incurred. These expenses are cost of warehouse space, utilities, working capital for the inventory, and labor.
2. Vendor will then have 30 days to remove the product from the warehouse. If the vendor or his representative does not move the product out in the allotted time then [*name of retailer*] will donate the product to a non-profit organization or destroy it and vendor will remit the original invoice cost to [*name of retailer*] or it may be deducted from the next payment to Vendor.

When an item has been an active item for six months or more [*name of retailer*] may in its discretion give Vendor or his representative written notice that it has elected to discontinue designated item and the manufacturer or his agent will have thirty (30) days to move the product out of the warehouse. After the allotted thirty (30) days the product will be donated to a non-profit organization or destroyed and Vendor will remit the original invoice cost to [*name of retailer*] or it may be deducted from the remit payment to the Vendor.

It is not our intent to penalize companies for introducing new items. It is our intent to recoup some of our cost and eliminate inventories when an item is not selling.

Understood and Signed:

[*name of retailer*]
By: _____
Its: _____

Vendor
By: _____
Its: _____

Wholesalers and retailers maintain that such fees are a rational response to changing economic conditions. As the number of new products multiplies faster than increases in store size, the value of the space inside the store grows in proportion. Most distributors believe that suppliers should be willing to pay the higher rent associated with the changing conditions that they, the suppliers, have played such a large role in creating. Suppliers point out, however, that these allowances have serious unintended consequences. Perhaps most critical is the likely impact on the smaller company. Given the reality of limited resources, many smaller suppliers cannot pay high prices for access to shelf space. Such an expenditure would come out of another part of the marketing budget—perhaps reducing R&D, and thus innovativeness, or increasing product price. In either case, the probable result is to disadvantage small firms further relative to their larger competitors. Smaller firms argue that larger suppliers are better able to absorb slotting fees and, furthermore, that their strong brand franchises virtually ensure them retail shelf space even without slotting allowances.

NEW PRODUCT INTRODUCTION COSTS

Because new product introductions lead to costs for so many participants in the expanded grocery channels—manufacturers, brokers, wholesalers, retailers, consumers—identifying and categorizing the total systemwide costs of these introductions is difficult. In fact, few efforts at estimating these costs have been attempted. Those that have been attempted are fragments of the total picture—say, a manufacturer's promotional budget for a new product campaign or the retail slotting allowance.

One recent study bears special mention, however. Deloitte and Touche (1990) conducted a research project sponsored by six of the leading grocery trade associations in the United States. The principal objective was to document the process and the costs of introducing and deleting a new product from the grocery system, at all levels of the system. Data were collected on a sample of forty-one 1988 product introductions in fifteen grocery companies from the grocery manufacturing, broker, wholesale, and retail sectors. The activities associated with new grocery product introductions (and deletions) were identified and studied and the costs of each of these activities measured. Although this study sheds light on several hitherto unknown areas, its results should not be extrapolated to the industry as a whole since neither the firms nor the products were randomly selected. The results do, however, provide a base, where none existed before, regarding the approximate magnitude of the expenses associated with new product introductions (or deletions).

Product introductions follow a twenty-four-step process from manufacturer research and development to retail shelf performance monitoring after the product is in distribution, according to the study. Manufacturers participate in eighteen of these twenty-four steps, brokers participate in seven, and retailers are involved in eleven (Table 2.5). However, manufacturer spending is dominated by just four of the eighteen activities: research and development, market analysis, introductory trade deals and allowances, and consumer advertising and promotion. The last two categories, for example, averaged $10.1 million, or 64 percent of total manufacturer grocery introduction costs. The first two categories together average 14 percent of total introduction costs. Thus, these four categories alone account for over three-fourths of all manufacturers introduction costs. The total cost of the eighteen manufacturer activities ranged from $378,000 per multiple SKU launched to $63.5 million. The average cost of a multiple SKU launch was $15.9 million. This compares with the average cost of introducing a single SKU of $4.7 million. Since a number of economies of scale are present when introducing more than one SKU – total spending for advertising stays virtually the same, for example, whether four or ten SKUs are introduced – manufacturers averaged 3.4 SKUs on each new introduction in this study. Table 2.6 details the same costs for brokers, wholesalers, and retailers.

Several comments are warranted to describe retailer costs. First, these costs must be separated into headquarters fixed costs, which averaged $144 per SKU, and store-level costs, variable generally according to number of stores in the retail organization. These store-level costs averaged $8.27 per SKU. When adjusted for number of stores per retail company, the total retail cost per new SKU averaged $810 (Table 2.6).

These estimates are not comprehensive; they omit a number of nonquantifiable items, some of them substantial: the increased costs of managing complex production schedules in manufacturing plants, additional warehouse and store reset costs, and the sales and profit cannibalization that often occurs as the sales and profits from current products are affected by the new introduction. Moreover, most capital costs – for new plant construction often necessary for new production, for example – are not included. Thus, it is likely that these costs far understate actual systemwide costs. They do, however, provide a workable framework from which to conduct more detailed analyses in the future.

CONSUMER AND MARKETPLACE ROLES

The consumer is the final arbiter of new product success. Among the many reasons already cited to explain the growth of new products, con-

Table 2.5
Activities in the Product Introduction Process, 1988

	Manufacturer	Broker	Wholesaler	Retailer
1. Research and development	×			
2. New product approval	×			
3. First stage market analysis	×			
4. Technical analysis	×			
5. Pricing analysis and theoretical product P&L development	×			
6. Development of promotion plan	×			
7. Development of consumer advertising and trade collateral materials	×			
8. Second stage market analysis	×			
9. Organize rollout	×	×		
10. Communicate to direct and/or brokered sales force	×	×		
11. Full scale production	×			
12. Call on headquarters and stores	×	×	×	×
13. Initial product evaluation by trade			×	×
14. Buying committee approval			×	×
15. Product merchandising decisions			×	×
16. New product implementation-communication	×	×	×	×
17. New product implementation-MIS			×	×
18. New product implementation-warehouse & distribution			×	×
19. New product implementation-store operations	×	×	×	×
20. Introductory trade deals and allowances	×			
21. Communicate to consumers	×		×	×
22. New product implementation-finance & accounting			×	×
23. Monitor product performance	×	×	×	
24. Modify product and promotional programs	×	×		

Source: Deloitte and Touche. *Managing the Process of Introducing and Deleting Products in the Grocery and Drug Industries* (1990).

sumer and marketplace changes are clearly the most powerful. This is part of an increasing marketing orientation for both manufacturers and retailers. A marketing orientation recognizes that identifying and satisfying consumers' needs is the surest way to marketplace success and profitability. Indeed, it is common today to hear both retailers and suppliers describe their businesses as consumer driven.

The challenge with following this strategy is that the consumer is a moving target (some argue a target moving at an increasing speed). Since at least the 1950s, manufacturers have strived to develop brands that meet the needs of various segments of consumers. In that earlier era, however, only a few segments were generally recognized, and, as a result, manufacturers were able to use mass media and similar market-

Table 2.6
Summary of Case Study Costs Observed in New Product Introductions

| Sector | Value | GROCERY | | | | | |
| | | Cost Per Event[1] | | | Cost Per SKU[2] | | |
		Low	High	Avg[3]	Low	High	Avg[3]
Manufacturer	$Millions	$0.4	$63.5	$15.9	$0.4	$21.2	$4.7
Broker	$000's	25.9	45.5	36.0	7.6	36.2	10.6
Wholesaler	$	240	15,600	1,310	230	1,200	370
Retailer	$	470	9,750	2,900	450	1,220	810

[1]Cost per event is the cost of introducing/deleting one or more SKUs occurring at the same time.
[2]Cost per SKU is the cost of introducing/deleting one SKU.
[3]Mean of components.

Source: Deloitte and Touche. *Managing the Process of Introducing and Deleting Products in the Grocery and Drug Industries* (1990).

ing approaches for their products. By the 1980s, however, changes in consumer demographic and psychographic (e.g., life-styles and opinions) characteristics were so marked, and thus so many more consumer segments defined, that even retailers began to base their strategies — store formats, product mixes, pricing policies — on consumer segmentation.

The changes in the U.S. consumer demographics are well documented: average age is increasing, women are entering the work force at unprecedented rates, the number of persons per household is falling, childbearing is postponed until society is more educated, and real per capita income has continued to rise. Attitudinal change accompanies these demographics. Consumers are busier as a result of these changes but have more money to spend. They are more diet and nutrition conscious and more educated, so they are more interested in information about the food they eat and the components of it: calories, fat content, sodium, fiber, calcium, sugar, and so on. These changes influence not just what we eat but how we eat. Convenience, always important, has become even more so. Fragmented life-styles and longer working schedules in many families have replaced traditional meal gathering by all-day-long snacking ("grazing," to use the industry jargon).

These considerable shifts in consumer behavior have been closely monitored by the food industry. The resulting expanded number of consumer segments that now are identified and effectively isolated explains a great deal of the increase in new products. Manufacturers, and to a lesser extent, retailers in their own perishables departments, have attempted to match the more exacting needs and preferences of ever more precise consumer segments by an ever greater outpouring of new products. Table 2.7 illustrates the large increases in health-related products introduced in recent years as manufacturers have attempted to capitalize on consumer interests in diet, health, and nutrition (Exhibit 2.5). One might argue that these marketers follow the marketing orientation too well. Of course, innovativeness for its own sake is hardly sufficient. For real new product success, the innovation must be one that ultimately succeeds with consumers in the marketplace.

Exhibit 2.5
New Product Lines and Health Issues

In 1989, the surgeon general of the United States released new guidelines for health. Oat bran, fiber, and fresh produce all rose to the fore as weapons to ward off cancer. The exercise and fitness craze that started with a bang at the beginning of the 1980s is still the rage among baby boomers and baby boomers' babies. Fat is out—lean is the only way to eat. How are the wishes of consumers and the wisdom of doctors met by food manufacturers? They become one of the major forces in product development.

Gorman's New Product News reveals that the number of calorie-reduced foods launched in 1989 (962) was more than double that of 1988, and those claiming reduced fat increased 127 percent to 626. More than 10 percent of the 9,192 new products introduced in 1989 were touted as reducing fat and/or calories.

With two out of three adults consuming "light" food and beverages, the food industry has had to scramble to keep up with the demand, and product line extensions run the gamut from Cremora Light coffee whitener (Borden Inc.) to Wonder Light sourdough bread (Ralston Purina's Continental Baking division). While dairy products accounted for 56 percent of the new "light" foods introduced in 1989, other categories included bakery foods, entrees, and processed meats. Perhaps the most unusual category to show a move to light versions was cat food, with Ralston Purina introducing Tender Vittles Lite soft moist cat food.

Introductions of products claiming to have no additives and/or preservatives also boomed. Among product line extensions that quickly gained favor with consumers were Kraft General Foods' Breyer's Natural Light Ice Milk and Pepsico's Frito Lay's Wild 'n' Mild Ranch Corn Chips.

What's next? *Prepared Foods New Products Annual 1990* suggests that the categories to watch in the 1990s are all natural (no additives or preservatives) and organic foods, which increased 43 percent over 1988 with a total of 140 new products launched.

Table 2.7
New Products Bearing Health Claims, 1987–1989

	1987	1988	1989	% change ('89–'90)
Reduced/low calorie/lite	432	475	962	+102.5%
Reduced/low fat	159	275	626	+127.7
All natural	206	215	274	+ 27.4
Reduced/low salt	281	202	378	+ 87.1
No additives/no preservatives	52	153	186	+ 21.6
Low/no cholesterol	70	126	390	+209.5
Added/high fiber	55	56	73	+ 30.4
Reduced/low sugar	120	52	188	+261.5
Added/high calcium	53	4	27	+575.0
Organic	—	98	140	+ 42.8

Note: Health claims category totals are not additive; new products may carry more than one health claim.

Source: Gorman's New Product News (Gorman Publishing Company, 1990).

Finally, it is important to recognize that new products impose substantial direct and indirect costs on consumers as well: higher information-processing costs, potential countereffects of competitive brand advertising, higher search costs, potential confusion about new products' characteristics and availability, and higher prices. On average, for example, new products over a ten-year period from 1978 to 1987 were 23 percent more expensive than the other items already in the category they joined (*Progressive Grocer,* December 1989, p. 22). Hence, new products affect consumers not only in fulfilling previously unmet needs but also in influencing the overall performance of the food distribution system.

FACTORS INFLUENCING NEW PRODUCT ACCEPTANCE

In attempting better to understand new product introduction as a process and to isolate the factors responsible for acceptance of new products by supermarket buyers and their eventual marketplace success, past research needs to be examined.

A number of studies have been conducted recently attempting to explain what makes a new product a success in any industry.[6] These investigations in general agree that the following factors are critical to new product success:

1. Product differential advantage: A unique product with superior qualities as perceived by consumers, while still maintaining good value (e.g., performance to cost ratio).

2. Understanding users' needs and preferences: A customer orientation, where marketing assists in shaping the concept and design of the product.

3. Strong launch effort: Considerable amounts of selling, promotion, and distribution.

4. Technological strength and synergy: A good fit between the new product's technology and the resources and skills of the firm.

5. Marketing synergy: A good fit of the marketing, selling force, and distribution needs of the product and the firm's marketing resources and skills.

6. Attractive market: A high-growth market—is one with good long-run growth potential and, ideally, weak competitors.

7. Top management commitment and support.

Despite general agreement on these criteria for new product success, the criteria fall far short of prescribing managerial action. The success factors in most instances describe the setting of the project. How, for example, is "marketing and technological synergy" created when none exists before? How does one even know when such synergy is created? Similarly, a high-growth market makes good intuitive sense but is generally beyond the control of the manager, except in rejecting a proposed product at the selection stage. Furthermore, although some of the factors are under the control of the new product manager—a strong marketing orientation and a strong promotional program, for example—the specific action required is not delineated. Exactly what does a manager do to become more consumer oriented or to conceive a superior product? Thus, although these generalized studies on new product success factors have been useful as broad background summaries, they do not provide much specific guidance as to how a manager should behave under various scenarios. Indeed, much of this sort of past new product research was so preoccupied with the big issues—strategy, synergy, technology—that the actual new product introduction process was ignored. The pivotal role of the trade buyer intermediary was virtually ignored.

Another strain of research explores new product introductions into grocery channels more specifically. This research may be separated into those projects with a public policy approach or with a managerial (or private firm) perspective. In the former group, the common conceptual theme has been the S-C-P paradigm using secondary sources of data.[7]

A valuable strain of literature examines new product acceptance from a strategic managerial perspective. First, though various pretest-market models attempting to predict sales performance of new products allude to the importance of distribution, these models treat the variable in an ad hoc way or not at all (Robinson, 1981). We summarize the few studies of new product introduction that take the perspective of the channel intermediary.

Grashof (1970) used three alternative computer simulations to examine hypothetical performance outcomes associated with alternative product addition and deletion criteria for one product category, dog food. Product newness emerged as the most important qualitative criterion in this research. Heeler, Kearney, and Mehaffey (1973) obtained data from one Canadian grocer wholesaler for sixty-seven new grocery product selection decisions in an attempt to model the selection process used by buyers. Although the results of this study were promising in identifying new products that did not merit further examination, the researchers concluded that a much larger database would be required before their initial findings could be confirmed. Subsequently, Montgomery (1973) used two different analytical techniques to model buyer reaction to a small set of hypothetical new products. Certain of his findings were consistent with those of the few past studies (e.g., advertising support was a significant predicator variable), but Montgomery noted the cumbersome nature of his analytical models for larger data sets.

Thus, studies examining supermarket buyers' new product decisions relied on either simulated experiments, accept-reject decisions for a limited number of items and product categories, or buyer reaction to hypothetical new products. Furthermore, though some recent research has examined the process by which retailers "select" the trade promotions they accept (Curhan and Kopp, 1986, 1987–88; Hardy, 1986; Levy, Webster, and Kerin, 1983), no new research has been conducted on the new product selection process in more than a decade. Given the surge of new products in the last ten years and their increasing economic importance, new research on this important topic using primary data is required.

SYSTEMWIDE ISSUES

The introduction of new products into the grocery distribution system is partially described by the spectrum of costs, procedures, and operational challenges that are given shape by new products for manufacturers, distributors, and consumers – processes already discussed. There is, however, a set of larger issues, specific to no single firm or even group of participants to the new product introduction process. These issues are of a systemwide nature. As such they are particularly difficult to evaluate. Indeed, even agreeing on the appropriate measures is often a problem. To illustrate, suppliers frequently point out that the rising number of new products stimulates competition and expands consumers' choice set. More variety is generally preferred to less. But according to Gorman (1990), nearly 11,000 new products were introduced in 1988. At what point does desired variety become excessive, costly waste? And, still more sensitive than developing appropriate measurers for this difficult question, who gets to decide?

Nevertheless, critics of new product proliferation make five basic allegations (summarized by Connor, 1981):

1. Product proliferation is deceptive because most new products are imitations or minor variants of existing products and are often marketed by the same large companies.

2. Proliferation contributes to inflation because new products often have higher price-quality ratios than existing substitutes.

3. Proliferation results in waste from self-canceling advertising and operating plants at suboptimal production levels.

4. Proliferation creates consumer confusion and undermines rational decision making by making trial purchases and personal evaluation costly.

5. Product proliferation creates or exacerbates competitive problems by strengthening product differentiation and raising entry barriers for more specialized potential entrants.

Welfare analyses of optimal product diversity lead to no clear-cut judgment of the net effects of proliferation. Schmalensee (1978) also argues that there are not necessarily too many products for a given market, though proliferation deters entry that could lead to lower prices. The greatest concern about proliferation should be in the product categories with very high levels of concentration. The main hope of increasing competition in these categories is from new entrants; however, extensive proliferation by incumbent firms may leave no profitable market niches for a new firm to occupy.

Marion (1986), however, summarizes many systemwide welfare analyses of the optimal level of product variety by stating that no clear-cut judgment of the net effect of proliferation can be determined.

Efficiency is another systemwide phenomenon issue that bears close examination as a result of the impacts of new product introduction. New product development and subsequent market introduction absorb enormous energy and resources in the grocery distribution system;

there are costs and benefits for manufacturers, distributors, and consumers. Yet comparatively little research has been conducted to determine how new product acceptance decisions are actually made by channel intermediaries. If decision making by system participants can be made more effective, resource utilization is improved and systemwide efficiency increases. Profits can be higher for channel members, and at the same time prices can be lower for consumers. In a recent study of slotting allowances and forward buying, two phenomena often accompanying new products, a prominent conclusion was that these practices seriously impair efficiency in the distribution system and, in fact, add costs that are absorbed by the consumer (Buzzell, Quelch, and Salmon, 1990).

NOTES

1. Among the best-known works from this area, and from which much of this section is drawn, are Wind (1982), Urban and Hauser (1980), Pessemier (1982), Hisrich and Peters (1984), and Kuczmarski (1988).

2. Although the only portfolio framework presented here for analysis is the one developed by BCG, other schemes are available, such as General Electric's strategic winners screen (Hofer and Schende, 1978, in Bagozzi, 1986, p. 687), Shell's directional policy matrix (Robinson et al., 1978, in Bagozzi, 1986, p. 683), and McKinsey's integrated method (Peters and Waterman, in Kotler, 1988).

3. For a more complete description of the BCG matrix model, see Bruce D. Henderson, *The Experience Curve Reviewed: The Growth Share Matrix or the Product Portfolio* (Boston: BCG, 1973).

4. Numerous full texts treat such organizational matters: Wind (1982), Urban and Hauser (1980), and Hisrich and Peters (1984).

5. For an illustration of Bayesian decisions to the product decision of the firm, see Green (1962, in Wind, 1982, p. 240).

6. See, for example, the British project, SAPPHO (Rothwell, 1972), Project NewProd in Canada (Cooper, 1980), and a number of studies over the last twenty years in the United States, for example, the Standford Innovation Project (Maidique and Zirger, 1984).

7. Some relevant studies in this stream are those by Adams and Yellen (1976), who studied the similarity of new products; Schmalensee (1978), who identified new product proliferation as an explicit manufacturer strategy to erect entry barriers; and Scherer (1979), who estimated the welfare effects of new product introductions. Connor (1981) has investigated relationships between manufacturer market structure and the number of new products (for elaboration of these studies, see Connor, Rogers, Marion, and Mueller, 1985). As in much of the structure-performance literature, the emphasis on the conduct dimension in these studies, especially of the intermediary-buyer, is minimal.

3

RESEARCH PROCESS

The previous two chapters laid out the general structural and environmental context in which new product introductions take place, as well as the managerial issues of dealing with new product introduction into the marketplace. The significant role a trade intermediary (or its representative, e.g., a trade buyer) plays in the successful market introduction is quite evident. Thus, research into an understanding of the trade buyer's decision process will offer benefits to both marketers and policy makers. This chapter discusses a conceptual framework useful for studying this decision process and appropriate research methods and describes the procedures we employed for collecting the data reported in this book.

CONCEPTUAL FRAMEWORK

We begin the process of new product introduction after the product has been designed, developed, and tested. The firm has identified a marketing strategy for marketplace introduction; the decisions on retail selling price, trade margins, advertising strategy – expenditure plans among various media, copy theme – couponing strategy, and sampling plans have been made. Armed with the information on the new product's strategic plans, the firm offers the product to the trade. The representative (hereafter called trade buyer) of the trading firm (e.g., wholesaler, grocery chain, or other) is presented with the information on the new product.

The product presentation is made to the buyer by the manufacturer representative or a broker, or, often, both. The information presented generally includes a physical item description or a sample, details of overall marketing strategy, and support given to the item, including price, various terms of trade, promotional plans, and results of marketing research. Then the buyer considers the information presented and evaluates the item's long-term potential.

The trade buyer makes several judgments before reaching a final recommendation. These include an evaluation of the attributes of the new product (e.g., its physical performance, marketing support offered by the vendor for the product, suitability to the customers of the outlets), as well as the expected profitability, both short term and long term, associated with stocking the new product. The short-term profit potential is gauged against the offer made by the vendor in the introductory period (the first three months or so), and the long-term profit potential will be assessed by considering the marketing support the vendor will offer. Based on these evaluations, the trade buyer makes a recommendation as to the acceptance, rejection, or hold status for the new product to the buying committee or the head buyer responsible for the final decision (depending on the structure of the intermediary organization). Typically, about 90 percent of the buyer's recommendations are accepted by the buying committee. Figure 3.1 depicts this process as a flowchart. The process of evaluation depends not only on several factors related to the product but also the individual characteristics of the buyer and the organizational characteristics of the buying organization of the channel intermediary.

Once the new product is stocked on the shelves, its sales progress and its effects on related existing products are monitored. After a reasonable period of time (say, twelve months), a review is made as to whether to continue carrying the new product or to withdraw it.

This description of the process suggests several measures for assessing the new product's viability from the trade buyer's viewpoint: direct evaluations of the attributes of the product, evaluations of the profit potential (short term and long term), and a later decision about whether to continue with the new product. These measures fall neatly into three categories: judgments, choice behaviors, and continuation decision. The judgments can be elicited using rating scales with seven or ten points, while the choice behavior is a variable with three categories (accept, reject, or hold). The continuation decision is a variable with two categories (yes or no).

An understanding of the determinants of these various aspects of the decision process is essential for marketers of new products in designing strategies to enhance the new product's success. Appropriate statistical relationships can be developed between the measures of the decision process and the characteristics of the product and the decision maker, as well as the organization. The suitable methods are multiple regression for the judgments on rating scales and logistic regression for the other two measures.

Figure 3.1
A Conceptual View of the New Product Acceptance Process

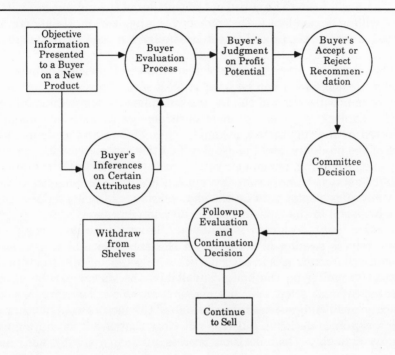

General Research Methods

Various research methods could be used to gain an understanding of the determinants of a new product's acceptance by a trade buyer and its success in the marketplace. We describe four methods in this section to set the stage for the research reported later: historical data analysis, field survey, conjoint analysis studies, and the delphi technique. The advantages and shortcomings of these methods differ from the perspective of the problem of new product acceptance under study. Prototypical data collection forms for the first three approaches are shown in the appendix to this chapter. They could be easily adapted to any actual application.

Historical Data Analysis. This approach involves collecting data on actual decisions (accept, reject, or hold) on the new products offered to a random sample of buying committees for a period of the past six months or so. The data on characteristics of products will also be collected from the historical files of the buying committees. Then statistical relationships can be developed that relate actual decisions to the characteristics of the products and buying committees. These historical data will probably be collected either by mail survey or by personal visits to the sites of the buying committees. In the case of a mail survey, data will have to be culled out of the files of the buying committee by a willing respondent in the trade buyer organization. If data are collected in person, the procedure will be similar, but the task of compiling the data can be handled by the individual visiting the site.

This approach offers the obvious advantage of utilizing data on actual decisions, but it can be fraught with several problems that arise due to noncooperation of the buying committees in providing data on decisions, lack of records on past decisions (particularly on products rejected by the committee), incompleteness of data on the characteristics of the products, and the usual difficulties associated with any survey (e.g., sampling, personnel costs, time involved in implementation). Additional disadvantages of this approach include an inability to collect any judgmental data on the characteristics of new products that will be useful in the modeling of the decision process.

Field Survey. A survey is conducted among a random sample of trade buyers seeking information on the importance of various new product characteristics in their decisions to accept or reject new products. Depending on the budget available, the survey can be implemented by mail, telephone, or a personal interview. The approach can quickly yield judgmental information on the factors contributing to the acceptance decision, but it is not clear that the trade buyers can clearly articulate their decision process in such a survey, and their judgments may not correspond to their actual decisions. Additional concerns with this approach include response and nonresponse errors, lack of assurance as to the common frame of reference employed by the respondents, and an inability to predict the acceptance probabilities for future products from these results. Nevertheless, this approach is highly suitable to supplement the data collected from historical records.

Conjoint Analysis. This approach involves seeking judgments from a sample of buyers on the acceptance or rejection of hypothetical new products. That is, rather than collecting data on decisions made on actual products, the researcher presents descriptions of hypothetical new products and obtains data on intended buyer behavior. By including a number of relevant characteristics and obtaining judgments on a fairly large number of hypothetical products, the method enables the determination of relationships between the accept or reject decision and the product characteristics.

This approach has been used in various studies on new product concept testing in marketing and has been useful in predicting marketplace behavior when the product concept is commercialized. As conjoint techniques have become more familiar and refined analytically, their use has greatly increased. Wittink and Cattin (1989), for example, found that commercial applications of conjoint analyses increased over 50 percent when comparing the five-year period between 1981 and 1985 with the total number of conjoint commercial applications conducted before this time. Moreover, since 1985, it is likely that use has become even more widespread with the development of commercially available software that makes conjoint techniques more accessible and has reduced the per-study cost substantially.

The conjoint method calls for expertise in the design or construction of the descriptions of new products. It also places a significantly high demand on the time of the respondent for providing the necessary judgments. However, with the emergence of software and new, refined data-gathering methods, conjoint methods offer much promise in the future of shedding light on new product introductions. A particularly fertile area of research will be the documentation of evidence that shows how conjoint analyses have validity in terms of their ability to predict trade buyer acceptance and marketplace success.

Delphi Technique. The delphi method is highly suitable for arriving at a consensus among a group of relevant decision makers, typically members of the buying committee, concerning new product acceptance.

In this method, each member is individually asked for his or her assessment of the degree of importance of various characteristics of a new product in gaining acceptance. These judgments are typically summarized by median importance scores. Then each member is given the summary information and is asked to revise his or her judgments if appropriate. The process is repeated two or three times until a consensus is reached. Experience with this method indicates that two iterations produce consensus in most situations. The method is useful in arriving at a common set of criteria for a buying committee. It is quite laborious to implement, particularly if information is sought from a large number of buying committees. It is useful as an exploratory device for research on the new product acceptance problem.

Research Steps Followed

Since there is no ideal research approach to tackle the problem under study, we adopted a combination of the methods noted in our research. This research was confined to one distributor firm rather than a sample of such firms. Here we outline the steps followed for collecting the data needed to develop the models.

Setting. Data were collected from a large supermarket chain whose headquarters and majority of stores are located in the northeastern United States. The chain is publicly held and covers a large trading area, with approximately 100 stores. Its 1986 sales approached $1 billion. The chain's headquarters region is one frequently employed by manufacturers for test marketing because of the representativeness of the consumer profiles and trading area. Hence, although the model developed here applies to only one company, the representativeness of the firm and its environment may permit a cautious generalization of the results to other market conditions. To evaluate new products, the retail firm in this study used a mix of individual buyer and committee.

Preliminary Interviews. We held several meetings with the head buyer and six individual buyers responsible for various departments in an effort to understand the mechanics followed within the chain for new product acceptance decisions. In addition to our extensive literature review of both academic and grocery industry trade sources, these meetings enabled us to identify the data sources readily available and any gaps that needed to be filled in by additional data collection. In a sense, the series of meetings could be deemed as a quasi-delphi process to reach some agreement on the parameters of the decision problem.

Research Approaches. We adopted a combination of research approaches: collection of historical data gathered concurrently with actual decisions made over a long period of time; a survey among individual buyers to obtain supplemental information on new products; collection of information on the status of new products accepted after two years; and conjoint analysis, in which buyers evaluated hypothetical profiles. We believe that this effort is unique and offers an immense opportunity to study the problem comprehensively.

Data on Actual Decisions. Three types of primary data were collected on actual decisions from the chain: vendor-supplied materials, including product physical characteristics, financial information, and promotional support; a one-page questionnaire completed by each buyer assessing qualitative attributes for every new item; and the final decision made by the buying committee. Figure 3.2 shows a preexisting form the retail company had used in the past. However, it became evident early in our meetings with the buyers that the existing data would not be adequate to capture their buying decisions. Trade buying is shaped not simply by the generally quantifiable data contained on Table 3.2, but by a variety of individual buyer judgments as well. How an ice cream actually tastes, the uniqueness of a particular packaging type, the track record of a particular vendor or the buyer's evaluation of the vendor's overall promotional efforts, and the effect of integrating the separate but related couponing, television advertising, and, perhaps, in-store merchandising. Figure 3.3 was developed to capture buyers' evaluations on these judgmental data.

Tables 3.1 and 3.2 provide information on the actual decision process and the interaction between the individual buyer and the buying com-

Figure 3.2
New Product Development Introduction Form

| Number Systems Designator | UPC Mfg. Code | UPC Item Code | Check Digit | UPC Case Code | ATTACH SAMPLE OF UPC LABEL IF POSSIBLE ON REVERSE SIDE |

PRESENTED TO: _____ BUYER _____ DATE OFFERED _____

ITEM DESCRIPTION _____ PACK ___ SIZE ___ DATE AVAIL _____

MANUFACTURER _____ ADDRESS _____ ZIP ___ PHONE _____

REPRESENTATIVE _____ ADDRESS _____ ZIP ___ PHONE _____

	PACK	SIZE ON LABEL	CASE COST DELIVERED	UNIT COST	SRP	% PROFIT	
REGULAR							
DEAL							

INTRODUCTORY OFFER _____

CASH DISC. _____ C.S. DIMENSIONS _____ CS/CU _____ CS WT. _____ PALLET _____

Case cost if sold FOB plant _____ FOB POINT _____ FRT. CS. _____ QTY. DISC. _____ LOCAL WHSE. _____ PICKUP ALWS. _____

MINIMUM ORDER _____ LEAD TIME _____ HOW SHIPPED _____ LIAB. INS. AMT. _____ CARRIER _____

STOCK PROTECTION POLICY _____ WHSL. _____ RETAIL _____ SALE GUARANTEE POLICY _____

CONFORMS TO F.D.A. _____ F.L.S.A. _____ HOW LONG ON MARKET _____ MGF. CODE DATING _____

SHELF LIFE _____ STATES WHERE PRODUCT IS TAXABLE _____ FOOD STAMP ELIGIBLE _____

VENDOR MASTERPACK _____ VENDOR INNER PACK _____ STATES THAT DO NOT ALLOW SALE ON SUNDAY _____

PREPRICED _____ DEPOSIT AMOUNT _____ DANGEROUS MATERIAL _____

MEDIA, AD DATES AND AREAS (Attach Schedule) _____

DISPLAY MATERIAL AVAILABLE _____

COOP. ADVTG., DATES, REQUIREMENTS _____

UNIT PRICE INFORMATION
WEIGHT (lb.)
LIQUID (qt.)
AREA (100 Sq. Ft.)
COUNT (per 100)

DIST. IN MKT.	RETAIL	DIST. IN MKT.	RETAIL	DIST. IN MKT.	RETAIL

THIS PRODUCT AND PROMOTIONAL ALLOWANCES ARE BEING PRESENTED TO ALL COMPETING CUSTOMERS IN THIS AREA ON A PROPORTIONALLY EQUAL BASIS.

SIGNED _____ DATE _____

Figure 3.3
Supplemental New Item Form

ITEM NAME:_____   BUYER INITIAL:_____
PRESENTATION MADE BY:_____
BROKER ONLY_____   COMPANY REP._____   BOTH_____
COMPETING STORES CARRYING THIS ITEM:_____

APPROXIMATE NUMBER OF
ITEMS WHICH DIRECTLY
COMPETE WITH THIS
ITEM ("ME-TOO" ITEMS)   BRANDS:_____

• Physical Attribute Performance (e.g., Taste and/or Effectiveness)	SUPERIOR 10 9 8		7	AVERAGE 6 5 4			3	INFERIOR 2 1		0		
• Package (e.g., Design, Color, Uniqueness)	SUPERIOR 10 9 8		7	AVERAGE 6 5 4			3	INFERIOR 2 1		0		
• Vendor Reputation (from Own Experience or Industry-wide)	SUPERIOR 10 9 8		7	AVERAGE 6 5 4			3	INFERIOR 2 1		0		
• Expected Performance (e.g., Growth) of Product Category (New Year)	SUPERIOR 10 9 8		7	AVERAGE 6 5 4			3	INFERIOR 2 1		0		
• Total Vendor Advertising/Promotion/ Support (including All Forms of Promotional Support in Short and Long Runs)	SUPERIOR 10 9 8		7	AVERAGE 6 5 4			3	INFERIOR 2 1		0		
• Total Profit Contribution Potential in Short Run (with Introductory Vendor Support)	SUPERIOR 10 9 8		7	AVERAGE 6 5 4			3	INFERIOR 2 1		0		
• Total Profit Contribution Potential in Long Run (with "Normal" Vendor Support (after Introductory Support is Withdrawn)	SUPERIOR 10 9 8		7	AVERAGE 6 5 4			3	INFERIOR 2 1		0		

---

mittee for both product additions and deletions. Table 3.1 lists the new item introduced, along with several key attributes and the actual committee decision for a sample of new products the buyer presented to the committee. Although approximately 90 percent of all decisions for new products are either "yes" or "no," several other decisions are possible: "hold for more information," "preorder," or, as in the case of Snow Floww Tomatoes, "In & Out during January."

Table 3.1
New Items Meeting: New Product Decisions

Decision	Pk/Size	Item	Cost/Intro.	Retail	Margin (Deal/Reg.)
No	12/15z	Hormel Chunky Chili	9.85/1.68	.99	17/31%
Yes	12/16z	Green Giant Niblets Corn, Peas, Mixed Veg.	8.82/1.84 6.98	.79	26%
Yes	12/8.5z	Van de Kamp Lt & Crispy Haddock	12.10/2.40	.99	18%
No	6/64z	Nature's Choice Fruit Punch Apple Juice	5.30	.99	11%
No	24/20z	DelMonte Pineapple Chunk, Crush	14.00	.69	15%
In & Out January	24/27z	Snow Floww Tomatoes Disc. 00945, 00947	11.00	.58	21%
Hold	6/20ct	Yellobags Trash Bags 1 w/1 up to 200 cases free + 1 w/3 for 45 days	12.83/1 w/1	2.88	26/44%
No	20/9z	Tasters Choice Regular Bonus Jar	101.16	4.98	−2%

Table 3.2 shows a computer report that the retailer in this study relied on for additional information when considering product deletions.
This company makes the deletion decision coincident with the new
item acceptance decision nearly 100 percent of the time. It employs a
rule of thumb that is widely accepted in the retail industry: one in, one
out. There is rarely adequate room to allow a net addition of products.
Furthermore, over 80 percent of the time, the item deleted comes from
the same general category as the new product introduced. This greatly
facilitates new shelf placement and merchandising in the store as well
as storage in the warehouse.

Table 3.2 provides the information considered when buyers make
suggestions to the buying committee, which has responsibility for the
ultimate decision regarding product deletions. Several of the products
listed in the table are different sizes of the same product with the same
brand name. The key variables are demand, gross profit percentage,
gross profit dollars, and deal amount off. The report can be read as
follows: Product A is a 32-ounce item that comes twelve to a case;
twenty-eight cases a week sell in an average thirteen-week period, at an
unadjusted case cost of $14.32 per case, a retail selling price of $1.59
per unit, a gross profit of 24.9 percent, and a total gross profit of
$133.28 per case per week.

When product true costs are adjusted for temporary manufacturer
promotional deals, however, their actual profitability can change

Table 3.2
Commodity Gross Profit Report, July 31, 1990

Item Size	Pack	Description	Demand	Gross Profit - % -	Sale Price	True Cost	Deal Off	Gross Profit - $ -
32 oz	12	Product A	28	24.9	$1.59	14.32	.00	133.28
96 oz	6	Product B	42	23.6	3.79	17.38	.00	225.12
96 oz	6	Product C	47	24.6	3.69	16.70	.00	255.68
128 oz	4	Product D	78	24.6	4.99	15.05	.00	382.98
64 oz	9	Product E	152	24.6	2.59	17.58	.00	870.96
64 oz	9	Product F	127	16.4	1.88	16.90	2.76	353.06
128 oz	4	Product G	85	24.5	4.89	14.77	.00	407.15
32 oz	16	Product H	41	.7	2.29	36.38	.00	10.66
96 oz	6	Product I	28	4.5	6.99	40.05	.00	52.92
96 oz	6	Product J	55	4.3	6.99	40.12	.00	100.10
64 oz	9	Product K	236	.3	4.49	40.30	.00	25.96
64 oz	9	Product L	199	.1	4.49	40.36	.00	9.95
64 oz	9	Product M	461	6.0	2.99	27.29	.36	746.82
96 oz	6	Product N	112	24.0	5.99	27.32	.00	965.44
64 oz	360	Product O	0	100.0	3.99	957.20	.00	.00
64 oz	9	Product P	238	6.0	2.99	27.29	.36	385.56
96 oz	6	Product Q	67	24.0	5.99	27.32	.00	577.54
64 oz	9	Product R	276	21.0	2.89	20.54	.36	1,509.72
32 oz	12	Product S	0	100.0	1.79	16.53	.00	.00
64 oz	6	Product T	0	100.0	3.39	15.70	.00	.00
32 oz	16	Product U	77	23.6	1.59	19.44	.36	462.00
128 oz	4	Product V	130	23.4	5.69	17.43	.36	692.90
96 oz	6	Product W	85	23.6	4.39	20.12	.36	528.70
64 oz	6	Product X	0	100.0	2.49	10.74	.00	.00
96 oz	4	Product Y	254	22.8	3.99	12.32	.00	924.56
64 oz	6	Product Z	485	22.9	2.79	12.90	.00	1,862.40

Source: Reprinted from *Journal of Marketing,* Published by the American Marketing Association, Chicago, IL 60606. V. R. Rao and E. W. McLaughlin, "Modeling the Decision to Add New Products by Channel Intermediaries," January 1989, Vol. 53.

greatly. In Product F, for example, there is a $2.76 deal per case for every case sold. Thus the relevant cost to subtract from total sales, $16.92 ($1.88 × 9), is the actual case cost including the deal, $14.14 ($16.90 − $2.76), yielding a $2.78 per case profit or a $353 gross profit per week for Product F when it is on this particular promotional program.

When trying to determine which product to eliminate from a category, buyers consider not only the gross profit percentage, or the weekly case movement (demand) in isolation but attempt to integrate the two. That is, a relatively low-demand item may be retained if it has a high gross profit rate, and vice versa.

Data Gathering and Coding. The data for both forms were collected for over 2,000 products on a weekly basis from June 1986 to February 1987. Although all the materials transmitted from the vendor to the retail company were collected and examined, the vendor-supplied materials were not uniformly complete or available for every product. Often, for example, information on test marketing, point-of-purchase materials, or advertising and promotional support were either not presented by the vendor or missing. Experienced coders evaluated the total packet of materials and developed a series of measures regarding the overall quality of the presentation and marketing plan proposed for the new item.

The data collection produced a number of variables where preliminary analyses were necessary before selection could be made regarding the appropriate measure to incorporate into subsequent modeling. The "Introductory Market Development Funds" attribute in Figure 3.4 was one such instance. Nine different types of promotional allowances and payment schemes were recorded under this attribute. The attributes were subjected to factor analysis to determine the most meaningful factors with a minimum of redundancy.

Data on Hypothetical Products. We identified a set of twelve attributes on which a new product can reasonably be described for the conjoint analysis component of this research. These attributes were identified from three essential sources: the literature review, which revealed a number of variables that possessed significant explanatory power from past studies; the statistical models developed for the field portion of this research, which pointed to certain critical variables; and the total number of variables collected, which were subjected to factor analysis. The factor analysis grouped together those variables that could be summarized more succinctly for modeling purposes into a small number of factors. These factors were added to those identified from the first two sources to yield the following attributes: profit margin, prior experience with the vendor, quality of product and package, price, product status, competition (firms and brands), vendor support

88 Decision Criteria

Figure 3.4
Data Collection Form Using Conjoint Analysis

Buyer: John Baker   Product Category: Preserves
Item Number: 35

        Consider the new item in the product category (indicated above) currently being offered for the first time to your company. Assume that the vendor (broker or manufacturing representative) made a satisfactory presentation of this product. Also assume that the category "Additional Introductory Market Development Funds" may be channeled at your discretion into any combination of non-price factors (e.g., free goods, in-store displays, off-invoice provisions, etc.). Assume further that the various non-price factors (e.g., case allowance, free goods, off-invoice provisions) are about average for the category.

        Based on the description below and your general knowledge of the category, please make an assessment regarding your expectation of the new product's profitability, vendor's marketing support, and, finally, your likely accept/reject recommendation.

Profit Margin	35%
Prior Experience with Vendor	HIGHLY UNFAVORABLE
Uniqueness (Product and Package)	OUTSTANDING
SRP Relative to Category	MUCH BELOW AVERAGE
Product Status	ENTIRELY NEW PRODUCT
Competing Firms Carrying the Item	0
Competing Brands Carried by the Chain	3
Vendor Support: TV Advertising	MUCH INFERIOR
Vendor Support: Coupons	OUTSTANDING
Test Market/Marketing Research Results	NOT CONVINCING
Presentation and P-O-P Materials	HIGH QUALITY
Additional Introductory Market Development Funds	BELOW AVERAGE

JUDGMENTS:

(a) What is your assessment of its likely profit potential?
Outstanding ☐   Above Average ☐   Average ☐   Below Average ☐   Much Inferior ☐

(b) How do you assess the strength of the marketing strategy support of the vendor?
Outstanding ☐   Above Average ☐   Average ☐   Below Average ☐   Much Inferior ☐

(c) What is your recommendation to the buying committee?
Accept ☐   Reject ☐   Hold ☐

in television advertising and coupons, test market and marketing research results, presentation of point-of-purchase materials, and additional introductory market development funds. The levels used for each of these attributes are shown in Exhibit 3.1. The data collection instrument is shown in Figure 3.4. Data on 875 new product descriptions covering a total of 25 product categories were collected from five buyers using this approach.

Exhibit 3.1
**Buyers' Evaluations of Hypothetical New Products: Ranges for
Each Attribute**

Product Category: Specific to one of the assigned categories to the buyer. Defined narrowly—
e.g., fruit juices.

A   Profit Margin: Five choices specific to the product category

       Vendor: [To be included in the scenario]

B   Prior Experience with Vendor: Highly Favorable; Favorable; Neutral (no experience);
Unfavorable; Highly Unfavorable

C   Uniqueness (Product and Package): Outstanding; Above Average; Average; Below
Average; Much Inferior

       Category Growth Rate Per Year: To be judged by the buyer for each category.

D   Price: Relative to the category

       Five Levels: Much Above Average; Above Average; About Average; Below Average;
Much Below Average

E   Product Status: Entirely New Product/Me-too Product/Line Extension of Size/Line
Extension of Pack/Line Extension of Formulation

F   Competing Firms Carrying the Item: 0, 1, 3, 6, 8

G   Competing Brands (Private Label and National) Carried by the Chain: 0, 1, 3, 6, 8

       Vendor Support

H   TV Advertising: Outstanding; Above Average; About Average; Below Average;
Much Inferior

I   Coupons: Outstanding; Above Average; Below Average; Much Inferior; Not Utilized

J   Test Market/Marketing Research Results: Highly Convincing; Moderately
Convincing; Not Convincing; Not Provided

K   Presentation and P-O-P Materials: Outstanding; High Quality; Low Quality; Much
Inferior Quality; Not Available

L   Additional Introductory Marketing Development Funds: Outstanding; Above
Average; Below Average; Much Inferior; Not Available

APPENDIX 3.A: PROTOTYPICAL DATA COLLECTION FORMS FOR THREE RESEARCH METHODS

HISTORICAL DATA ANALYSIS

The data collection form for this method entails information on various characteristics of the new item presented to the buyer and the final decision. The information collected is naturally constrained by what has been kept in the records of the firm.

The form will be quite specific to the firm used for study. For each new product the main aspects to be collected are as follows:

> Product Name:
> Product Category:
> Suggested Retail Price Per Unit:
> Gross Margin—Normal:
> Gross Margin—Introductory:
> Terms of Trade:
> Minimum Order Quantity:
> Discount Structure:
> Introductory Incentives:
> Details of Marketing Support Offered by Vendor:

Decision:　　☐　Accept　　　☐　Reject

　　　　　　　☐　Hold　　　　☐　In & Out

FIELD SURVEY

In this method, a sample of trade buyers will be asked to rate the degree of importance of various characteristics of new products in their decision to accept or reject the new product.

The basic form will contain the following information.

1. Who makes the decision to accept/reject the new product?　　Buyer　　　　　　　☐
　　　　　　　　　　　　　　　　　　　　　　　　　　　　Buying Committee　☐
　　　　　　　　　　　　　　　　　　　　　　　　　　　　Other　　　　　　　☐

2. Rate each of the following characteristics on a 1 (Low) to 10 (High) scale to indicate its relative importance in your decision to accept or reject a new item.

    (a) Product Newness:　　　　　　　　1 2 3 4 5 6 7 8 9 10

(b) Physical Aspects of the Product: 1 2 3 4 5 6 7 8 9 10

(c) Relative Importance of the Item   1 2 3 4 5 6 7 8 9 10
    (relative to average of the category):

(d) Expected Product Category Growth: 1 2 3 4 5 6 7 8 9 10

(e) Vendor Support: 1 2 3 4 5 6 7 8 9 10

(f) Your Firm Being the First to Accept   1 2 3 4 5 6 7 8 9 10
    the Product:

(g) Terms of Trade Offered (for each of a   1 2 3 4 5 6 7 8 9 10
    set of terms of trade—slotting
    allowances, free cases, bill back, etc.):

(h) Synergy Offered by the New Item: 1 2 3 4 5 6 7 8 9 10

(i) Presence of Brands Competing with   1 2 3 4 5 6 7 8 9 10
    the New Item:

(j) Gross Margin: 1 2 3 4 5 6 7 8 9 10

(k) Profit per Unit of Resources   1 2 3 4 5 6 7 8 9 10
    Committed:

3(a) How many new products are offered to
your firm per week on the average?

(b) How many of these do you normally
accept?   _____

CONJOINT ANALYSIS

This questionnaire will look quite similar to the one shown in Figure 3.4.

4

PROFILE OF NEW PRODUCTS

This chapter presents the descriptive data on the characteristics of the two major new product types discussed in Chapter 3: actual products and hypothetical products. In the former category, the emphasis of the chapter, new product profiles are constructed using historical secondary information as well as new primary data. The hypothetical profiles are developed using our own primary data.

NEW PRODUCT INTRODUCTIONS: A SUPPLIER VIEW

There are a number of sources on recent trends in new product introductions by grocery suppliers into the grocery distribution systems. A. C. Nielsen, *Progressive Grocer,* and Marketing Intelligence Services regularly or occasionally present statistical trends, as well as product descriptions and industry commentary on various aspects of new product introductions. Perhaps the most comprehensive source, including the most consistent data set on new product introductions, is *New Product News.*

Table 4.1 shows the new product introductions as tracked by *New Product News (NPN)* for the period from 1985 to 1989. Several noteworthy trends are illustrated in this table. First is the sheer magnitude of the number of new products introduced each year: 12,055 in 1989 alone – and this does not include new package sizes, new ingredients or formulations, or product improvements. *NPN* defines a new product as an addition to the consumer product line of a manufacturer that is either a new brand or a new extension (e.g., new flavor or variety) of an existing brand – that is, something the supplier is providing for the first time. Second, the number of new products introduced has risen in each of the most recent five years. The number of new products introduced annually grew fourfold from the yearly average in the 1970s and increased 14 percent between 1988 and 1989 alone. Third, there is a great variation in new product activity by category. Whereas there were 1,701 new condiments (sauces, spices, and dressings) introduced in 1989, there were only 53 new baby foods. Finally, although Table 4.1 reports both food and nonfood grocery introductions, food consistently accounts for slightly more than three-fourths of all new introductions.

Table 4.1
New Grocery Product Totals, by Category, 1985–1989

Food categories:	1985	1986	1987	1988	1989
Baby foods	14	38	10	55	53
Bakery foods	553	681	931	968	1155
Baking ingredients	142	137	157	212	233
Beverages	625	697	832	936	913
Breakfast cereal	56	62	92	97	118
Candy/gum/snacks	904	811	1145	1310	1355
Condiments	1146	1179	1367	1608	1701
Dairy	671	852	1132	854	1348
Desserts	62	101	56	39	69
Entrees	409	441	691	613	694
Fruits and vegetables	195	194	185	262	214
Pet food	103	80	82	100	126
Processed meat	383	401	581	548	509
Side dishes	187	292	435	402	489
Soups	167	141	170	179	215
TOTAL	**5,617**	**6,107**	**7,866**	**8,183**	**9,192**
Non-food categories:					
Health and beauty aids	1,446	1,678	2,039	2,000	2,308
Household supplies	184	178	161	233	372
Paper products	42	42	47	100	121
Tobacco products	27	27	51	12	29
Pet products	14	9	18	30	33
TOTAL, NON-FOOD	**1,713**	**1,934**	**2,316**	**2,375**	**2,863**
GRAND TOTAL	**7,330**	**8,042**	**10,182**	**10,558**	**12,055**

Source: Gorman's New Product News (Gorman Publishing Company, 1990).

New product introductions are not evenly distributed throughout the year. Generally there are two periods when introductions are more concentrated: April-May, to get into advantageous position for summer sales of seasonal products, and July-August, to prepare for the back-to-school market. In 1989, 43 percent of all products were introduced during these four months alone (Table 4.2). By contrast, in January, only 637 products were introduced—just 5 percent of annual introductions—apparently due to consumers' lack of propensity to spend after the holiday period. Not all categories adhered to this average. Dessert suppliers introduced only 30 percent of their new products, for example, during the four-month peak period for companies in other categories (Table 4.3).

Table 4.4 shows the twenty suppliers that led in new product introductions in 1988–89. It appears that innovativeness by large brand manufacturers tends to be a constant process, at least in terms of new product introductions. Seventeen of the twenty leaders in 1988 were also leaders in 1989. The Philip Morris Corporation, including its Kraft and General Foods divisions, introduced 332 new products in 1989. However, it is significant to note that of all new food products introduced, the large manufacturers still account for only a minority. From 1985 to 1989, consistently over 80 percent of all new products introduced came from companies other than the leading twenty. In 1989, 83.12 percent of all new products were introduced by companies that were generally not in the group of the largest U.S. food manufacturers (Table 4.5).

The evidence appears to reinforce the popularly held notion that most truly new ideas come from small and medium-sized companies,

Table 4.2
New Product Introductions, by Month, 1985–1989

	1985	1986	1987	1988	1989
January	382	445	552	602	637
February	652	778	812	875	836
March	598	650	979	967	1015
April	539	634	809	1071	1170
May	666	838	1031	883	1239
June	608	692	684	667	937
July	777	814	1016	1129	1360
August	684	748	1049	1042	1361
September	505	582	786	724	849
October	645	611	737	829	1060
November	714	698	972	1138	863
December	560	552	757	638	728
TOTAL	**7,330**	**8,042**	**10,182**	**10,558**	**12,055**

Source: Gorman's New Product News (Gorman Publishing Company, 1990).

Table 4.3
New Product Totals, by Category and Month, 1989

Category	Jan	Feb	Mar	Apr	May	Jun	Jul	Aug	Sep	Oct	Nov	Dec	Total
Food categories:													
Baby foods	1	5	0	1	7	0	6	12	0	21	0	0	53
Bakery foods	38	72	121	123	86	122	102	144	130	71	84	62	1155
Baking ingredients	13	26	46	25	10	5	21	23	30	14	5	15	233
Beverages	51	59	66	116	67	95	112	102	56	74	45	70	913
Breakfast cereal	6	8	5	16	17	0	8	11	11	18	10	8	118
Candy/gum/snacks	54	118	136	116	139	84	135	253	97	105	69	49	1355
Condiments	66	153	159	219	179	109	238	287	69	72	65	85	1701
Dairy	83	82	72	104	225	149	95	157	102	92	140	47	1348
Desserts	2	6	9	6	2	10	2	11	7	5	2	7	69
Entrees	57	71	120	53	70	16	41	19	61	90	48	48	694
Fruits and vegetables	21	9	18	34	20	4	7	36	11	36	13	5	214

Pet food	6	4	4	11	10	12	8	26	15	6	9	15	126
Processed meat	21	32	37	69	52	42	50	45	31	35	47	48	509
Side dishes	39	21	41	42	46	30	50	35	21	32	111	21	489
Soups	6	10	13	30	36	1	19	54	13	21	3	9	215
Total, food	464	676	847	965	966	679	894	1215	654	692	651	489	9192
Non-food categories:													
Health and beauty aids	144	117	143	184	200	226	369	111	156	317	177	164	2308
Household supplies	12	27	17	5	59	26	84	12	21	22	24	63	372
Paper products	11	12	5	3	6	4	9	14	16	24	8	9	121
Tobacco products	2	4	3	0	0	2	3	8	2	3	0	2	29
Pet products	4	0	0	13	8	0	1	1	0	2	3	1	33
Total, nonfood	173	160	168	205	273	258	466	146	195	368	212	239	2863
Grand total	637	836	1015	1170	1239	937	1360	1361	849	1060	863	728	12,055

Source: *Gorman's New Product News* (Gorman Publishing Company, 1990).

Table 4.4
New Food Products by Company, 1988–1989

	Company	1989	1988	% Change
1.	Philip Morris	332	253	+ 31%
2.	Campbell Soup	156	78	+100%
3.	Nestle	115	99	+ 16%
4.	Borden	104	77	+ 35%
5.	Heinz	92	106	– 13%
6.	ConAgra	89	69	+ 29%
7.	Ralston Purina	77	49	+ 55%
8.	RJR Nabisco	75	56	+ 34%
*9.	Lever-Lipton	66	29	+127%
10.	Pillsbury	56	50	– 12%
11.	Beatrice	53	62	– 15%
12.	M&M/Mars	50	41	+ 22%
13.	General Mills	44	69	– 36%
14.	Pet	42	40	+ 5%
*15.	CPC International	39	21	+ 86%
16.	Sara Lee	38	56	– 32%
17.	Quaker Oats	32	50	– 36%
*18.	Wessanen USA	31	22	+ 41%
19.	Dean Foods	29	37	– 22%
20.	Geo. A. Hormel	29	34	– 18%
	Total	**1,549**	**1,298**	**+ 19%**

*New to listing. They replace McCormick (1988, 33; 1989, 23) and Cadbury-Schweppes (1988, 31; 1989, 8).

Source: Gorman's New Product News (Gorman Publishing Company, 1990).

despite a recent laboratory market plan developed for an ideal national introduction of a new product that totaled $54 million, not including development costs (*NPN,* July 7, 1989). Many marketers contend that large companies cannot afford the risk of a major product failure and consequently are more conservative and less innovative. The ability of

Table 4.5
New Food Product Introductions by Top Twenty Companies, 1985-1988

	1985	1986	1987	1988	1989
Total foods	5617	6107	7866	8183	9192
Top 20 total	1039	1137	1391	1290	1549
Top 20 (%)	16.2	18.5	18.6	15.8	16.9%
Other (%)	83.8	81.5	81.4	84.2	83.1%

Source: Gorman's New Product News (Gorman Publishing Company, 1990).

smaller companies to remain active in new product innovation and introduction will depend in large measure on the industry's response to
the slotting allowance dilemma discussed in Chapter 2. If current promotional fund requirements continue or if slotting fees escalate, the
future participation of smaller firms in new product introductions will
certainly become more difficult and, in many instances, may be
precluded.

NEW PRODUCT INTRODUCTIONS: A RETAILER VIEW

To gain perspective on the extent of the role that new products play
in retail operations, a number of key indicators can be examined. An
important set of such indicators emerges from a 1987 study conducted
by *Progressive Grocer* cooperatively with Super Valu, a Minneapolis-
based grocery wholesaler. In 1989, Super Valu was the nation's largest
voluntary grocery wholesaler. *Progressive Grocer* (*PG*) compared new
product data compiled from Super Valu's wholesale warehouse with
data collected from a similar *PG* study in the same warehouse in 1978.
Although the data came from one company only, because Super Valu is
one of the largest grocery wholesalers in the United States, the profile
of new products is likely to be fairly representative of the larger universe of U.S. wholesale and chain grocery warehouses.

In the period between the two *PG* studies (1978-87), the number of
total products in the grocery warehouse grew from 5,990 to 8,053 (34.4
percent). This excludes all fresh food departments, such as meats, fish,
produce, and deli. The variations in individual categories are substantial. Dietetic products shrank from 96 in the earlier study to 24 in 1987;
the number of dried vegetables grew 340 percent over the period, from
40 to 176 (Table 4.6).

Table 4.6
Total Warehouse Grocery Items, 1978 and 1987

	Total Number of Items		% change 1987 vs. 1978
	1987	1978	
Baby Foods	243	236	3.0%
Baking mixes	210	224	−6.3
Baking needs	241	152	58.6
Beverage powders, bases	113	116	−2.6
Breakfast foods	357	199	79.4
Candy, gum	974	876	11.2
Cigarettes	253	117	116.2
Coffee, tea, cocoa	368	167	120.4
Condiments	58	48	20.8
Cookies	123	105	17.1
Desserts	170	155	9.7
Dietetic	24	96	−75.0
Fish, canned	78	49	59.2
Fruit, canned	189	143	32.2
Fruit, dried	12	33	−63.6
Household cleaning	200	200	N.C.
Household supplies	125	126	−0.8
Jams, jellies, spreads	195	186	4.8
Juices, drinks	234	136	72.1
Laundry supplies, soap	533	394	35.3
Milk, powdered and canned	14	25	−44.0
Nuts	149	77	93.5
Paper products, wraps	433	272	59.2
Pasta	179	65	175.4
Pet Foods	432	281	53.7
Pickles, olives, relish	129	123	4.9
Prep. foods, canned meat	226	253	−10.7
Salad dressings, mayo	188	129	45.7
Sauces, sauce mixes	226	144	63.7
Seasonings, spices	262	230	13.9
Shortenings, oils	64	35	82.9
Snacks	127	69	84.1
Soft drinks	103	80	28.8
Soups	261	150	57.5
Sugar	31	23	34.8
Syrup	49	36	36.1
Vegetables, canned	304	200	52.0
Vegetables , dried	176	40	340.0
Total	8,053	5,990	34.4

Source: Super Valu/Progressive Grocer research (December 1987).

These figures are not strictly comparable to the total new product introductions discussed in the previous section for several reasons. First, only one company is being examined. Second, new sizes are counted as a different product by the *PG* study but not by *NPN*. Third, all direct products that circumvent the warehouse, that is, those delivered directly to the store (DSD), which may represent 25 percent of the total products in a supermarket, are not included. Finally, not all categories in the *NPN* are located in the warehouse studied.

Table 4.7 presents a review of selected indexes for all products in the *PG* study. The average suggested retail price of these 8,053 items was $1.43 in 1987 as compared to an average price per item of $.78 in 1978 ($1.23 in 1987 dollars, adjusted for inflation). Further, the gross margin average for all categories was 21.1 percent in the earlier study versus 28.9 percent in the more recent study. Thus, both retail price and gross margin have continued to grow.

The role of new products within the framework of the entire wholesale-retail portfolio of products has become increasingly important (Table 4.8). In 1987 products introduced during the proceeding ten years accounted for nearly half (47.2 percent) of all unit grocery sales and slightly greater than half (52.3 percent) of total grocery dollar sales. Moreover, 65.3 percent of all grocery products stocked in the warehouse have been introduced in the last ten years. Of course, many of these "new" products reflect necessary places in the warehouse for new package sizes, new flavors, and minor product improvements. *NPN* (July 7, 1989) estimated that by eliminating all changes but those fundamental to defining a truly new product, brand, or category would reduce the number of new product introductions in 1987 from 7,886 to 407. According to this procedure, perhaps as little as 5 percent of all product changes in the warehouse and store can fairly be described as truly new. Although less favorable demand conditions and new cost-reducing technologies have resulted in net reductions in the price for some new items relative to competing items already established in the category, these products are the exceptions. Overall, when the prices of new products were compared to those of other products in the same categories already on the shelves, the prices of the new items were, on average, 23 percent higher. Further, while over half of all grocery sales are generated by products new in the ten previous years, only thirteen of the thirty-eight categories (34 percent) have a sales ratio of new items to total items this high (Table 4.9). This is explained by noting that the largest sales categories (candy and gum, paper products, and laundry supplies and soaps) were most active in new product activity between 1978 and 1987. Only about 30 percent of the 1978 sales were produced by products introduced in the five prior years (*PG*, December 1987, p. 28). However, thirty-one of the thirty-eight categories in 1987

Table 4.7

Total Warehouse Grocery Items: Numbers, Sales, Movement, Margin Shares, and Average Price, 1987

	All Items		Total			Margins	
	Number	% of total	% of units	% of dollars	% margin	Share of margin $	Avg. price
Baby Foods	243	3.02	2.93	1.92	22.6	1.55	$ .93
Baking mixes	210	2.61	1.90	1.90	29.2	2.16	1.43
Baking needs	241	2.99	2.77	3.10	30.8	3.57	1.60
Beverage powders, bases	113	1.40	1.70	1.12	28.3	1.22	.94
Breakfast foods	357	4.43	5.99	9.36	26.7	8.58	2.23
Candy, gum	974	12.09	6.01	4.29	34.4	5.62	1.02
Cigarettes	253	3.14	.74	6.16	8.8	1.80	11.96
Coffee, tea, cocoa	368	4.57	1.84	5.06	24.7	4.06	3.94
Condiments	58	.74	1.08	1.06	30.9	.95	1.40
Cookies	123	1.53	1.00	.98	32.6	1.18	1.40
Desserts	170	2.11	2.44	1.32	28.4	1.42	.77
Dietetic	24	.30	.10	.18	32.7	.20	2.52
Fish, canned	78	.97	2.44	2.22	27.7	2.40	1.30
Fruit, canned	189	2.35	2.67	2.00	30.0	2.32	1.07
Fruit, dried	12	.15	.05	.06	30.5	.07	1.99
Household cleaning	200	2.48	1.43	1.78	30.5	2.02	1.78
Household supplies	125	1.55	.67	.92	28.7	1.01	1.95
Jams, jellies, spreads	195	2.42	1.33	2.25	29.8	2.18	2.41
Juices, drinks	234	2.91	2.59	2.95	27.5	3.00	1.63
Milk, powdered and canned	14	.17	.46	.42	24.2	.36	1.20
Nuts	149	1.85	.73	1.17	29.4	1.29	2.29
Paper products, wraps	433	5.38	9.68	8.40	27.8	8.79	1.24
Pasta	179	2.22	3.63	2.25	29.3	2.37	.89
Pet Foods	432	5.36	5.19	4.60	29.9	5.04	1.27
Pickles, olives, relish	129	1.60	1.08	1.20	32.3	1.52	1.59
Prep. foods, canned meat	226	2.82	3.35	2.86	30.8	3.26	1.22
Salad dressings, mayo	188	2.33	1.69	1.84	31.5	1.99	1.55
Sauces, sauce mixes	226	2.81	3.70	2.90	30.9	3.27	1.12
Seasonings, spices	262	3.25	1.27	1.43	34.7	1.72	1.62
Shortenings, oils	64	.79	.77	1.27	28.8	1.24	2.36
Snacks	127	1.58	1.77	1.69	33.3	2.06	1.36
Soft drinks	103	1.28	4.19	3.10	28.9	3.62	1.06
Soups	261	3.24	7.36	3.35	27.5	3.29	.65
Sugar	31	.38	1.12	1.23	19.3	.77	1.57
Syrup	49	.62	.40	.65	28.4	.68	2.36
Vegetables, canned	304	3.77	7.28	3.67	32.0	4.63	.72
Vegetables , dried	176	2.19	1.54	1.52	32.2	1.80	1.40
Total	8,053	100.00	100.00	100.00	28.9	100.00	$1.43

Source: Ibid.

Table 4.8
New Item Contribution to Warehouse Groceries and Price/Ratios, 1987

	New items as % of total category	New item sales		New items as % of margin $	New vs. old	
		% of units	% of dollars		Avg. price ratio	% margin ratio
Baby Foods	35.0	18.9	37.7	36.5	2.59	.88
Baking mixes	48.6	31.7	33.7	33.0	1.09	.96
Baking needs	52.7	35.2	39.2	39.9	1.18	1.00
Beverage powders, bases	83.2	45.1	43.0	42.3	.92	.96
Breakfast foods	72.3	57.7	60.0	62.0	1.10	1.09
Candy, gum	78.6	63.3	66.4	65.5	1.15	.99
Cigarettes	56.9	60.9	61.6	65.1	.89	.91
Coffee, tea, cocoa	78.3	60.9	61.6	65.1	1.03	1.11
Condiments	55.2	37.3	42.0	42.9	1.22	.99
Cookies	67.5	45.3	41.0	44.2	.84	1.06
Desserts	51.8	46.5	44.5	43.3	.92	1.00
Dietetic	62.5	72.2	84.8	82.7	2.15	.89
Fish, canned	69.2	34.7	36.9	36.7	1.10	1.06
Fruit, canned	60.3	47.2	49.3	50.0	1.09	1.03
Fruit, dried	25.0	21.1	12.7	14.2	.54	1.11
Household cleaning	57.5	47.1	50.1	49.6	1.13	.98
Household supplies	65.6	57.5	61.2	60.9	1.17	1.16
Jams, jellies, spreads	39.5	27.8	27.4	27.3	.98	.90
Juices, drinks	77.8	58.9	61.5	64.4	1.16	1.12
Laundry supplies, soap	87.6	82.2	88.3	87.4	1.63	.95
Milk, powdered and canned	50.0	9.6	23.4	24.1	2.87	.98
Nuts	73.2	69.5	71.9	70.9	1.12	.92
Paper products, wraps	78.5	64.5	63.0	63.2	.94	.88
Pasta	64.8	34.5	38.0	41.4	1.15	1.03
Pet Foods	73.4	61.2	63.4	63.5	1.10	.99
Pickles, olives, relish	41.9	31.2	29.8	31.4	.93	1.09
Prep. foods, canned meat	57.1	38.2	36.9	39.0	.95	.99
Salad dressings, mayo	63.3	52.7	54.9	57.5	1.09	1.06
Sauces, sauce mixes	63.3	39.7	47.2	48.0	1.36	1.03
Seasonings, spices	31.7	25.1	24.1	24.7	.95	.90
Shortenings, oils	64.1	52.7	48.8	49.6	.86	.98
Snacks	82.7	62.5	71.9	71.1	1.53	.94
Soft drinks	80.6	48.2	49.3	48.0	1.04	.98
Soups	58.2	22.4	29.4	32.2	1.45	1.03
Sugar	58.1	58.5	36.1	30.0	.40	.83
Syrup	63.3	43.9	48.2	49.5	1.19	1.07
Vegetables, canned	44.1	25.7	24.2	23.8	.92	.99
Vegetables, dried	59.7	56.5	54.0	55.9	.90	1.05
Total	65.3	47.2	52.3	52.8	1.23	.99

Source: Ibid.

Table 4.9
New Item Sales and Movement, 1978 and 1987

Rank 1987	Rank 1988	New items as % of $ sales		Rank 1987	Rank 1978	New items as % of unit sales	
1	4	88.3	Laundry supplies, soap	1	4	82.2	Laundry supplies, soap
2	28	84.8	Dietetic	2	32	72.2	Dietetic
3	22	71.9	Nuts	3	13	69.5	Nuts
4	3	71.9	Snacks	4	7	64.5	Paper products, wraps
5	2	66.4	Candy, gum	5	2	63.3	Candy, gum
6	6	63.4	Pet foods	6	3	62.5	Snacks
7	8	63.0	Paper products, wraps	7	8	61.2	Pet foods
8	23	62.5	Juices, drinks	8	28	60.9	Coffee, tea, cocoa
9	29	61.6	Coffee, tea, cocoa	9	23	58.9	Juices, drinks
10	15	61.2	Household supplies	10	21	58.5	Sugar
11	12	60.0	Breakfast foods	11	16	57.7	Breakfast foods
12	30	54.9	Salad dressings, mayo	12	11	57.5	Household supplies
13	38	54.0	Vegetables, dried	13	38	56.5	Vegetables, dried
14	10	40.1	Household cleaning	14	28	52.7	Salad dressings, mayo
15	27	49.3	Fruit, canned	15	33	52.7	Shortening, oils
16	9	49.3	Soft drinks	16	6	48.2	Soft drinks
17	35	48.8	Shortenings, oils	17	25	47.2	Fruit, canned
18	37	48.2	Syrup	18	10	47.1	Household cleaning
19	19	47.2	Sauces, sauce mixes	19	30	46.5	Desserts
20	33	44.5	Desserts	20	5	45.3	Cookies, crackers
21	1	43.0	Beverage powders, bases	21	1	45.1	Beverage powders, bases
22	18	42.0	Condiments	22	35	43.9	Syrup
23	7	41.0	Cookies, crackers	23	24	43.2	Cigarettes
24	25	40.3	Cigarettes	24	19	39.7	Sauces, sauce mixes
25	24	39.2	Baking needs	25	18	38.2	Prep. foods, canned meats
26	32	38.0	Pasta	26	20	37.3	Condiments
27	36	37.7	Baby foods	27	14	35.2	Baking needs
28	16	36.9	Fish, canned	28	27	34.7	Fish, canned
29	21	36.9	Prep. foods, canned meats	29	31	34.5	Pasta
30	20	36.1	Sugar	30	17	31.7	Baking mixes
31	17	33.7	Baking mixes	31	15	31.2	Pickles, olives, relish
32	13	29.8	Pickles, olives, relish	32	22	27.8	Jams, jellies, spreads
33	14	29.4	Soups	33	25	25.7	Vegetables, canned
34	11	27.4	Jams, jellies, spreads	34	36	25.1	Seasonings, spices
35	26	24.2	Vegetables, canned	35	12	22.4	Soups
36	31	24.1	Seasonings, spices	36	9	21.1	Fruit, dried
37	34	23.4	Milk, powdered and canned	37	37	18.9	Baby foods
38	5	12.7	Fruit, dried	38	34	9.6	Milk, powdered and canned

Source: Ibid.

generated 50 percent of their sales from new items. Margins for new and old products remained about the same.

Finally suppliers and retailers have apparently considered shifting their pricing strategies for new products in certain categories. Table 4.10 shows that when the price of new entries is compared to the prices of established competitors in the category, the ranking changes substantially between 1978 and 1987.

STATISTICAL DESCRIPTION FOR SAMPLE OF ACTUAL NEW PRODUCTS

The research project carried out in cooperation with the major grocery wholesaler-retail described in Chapter 3 produced extensive data

Table 4.10

New Products as a Percentage of Total Category and Rank, 1978 and 1987

Rank		New items as % of total category		Rank		Avg. price ratio new items vs. old	
1987	1988			1987	1978		
1	3	87.6	Laundry Supplies, soap	1	10	2.87	Milk, powdered and canned
2	1	83.2	Beverage powders, bases	2	10	2.59	Baby foods
3	4	82.7	Snacks	3	2	2.15	Dietetic
4	11	80.6	Soft drinks	4	18	1.63	Laundry supplies, soap
5	2	78.6	Candy, gum	5	33	1.53	Snacks
6	6	78.5	Paper products, wraps	6	23	1.45	Soups
7	26	78.3	Coffee, tea, cocoa	7	12	1.36	Sauces, sauce mixes
8	22	77.8	Juices, drinks	8	8	1.22	Condiments
9	7	73.4	Pet foods	9	30	1.19	Syrup
10	23	73.2	Nuts	10	35	1.18	Baking needs
11	16	72.3	Breakfast foods	11	26	1.17	Household supplies
12	12	69.2	Fish, canned	12	6	1.16	Juices, drinks
13	5	67.5	Cookies, crackers	13	26	1.15	Candy, gum
14	9	65.6	Household supplies	13	22	1.15	Pasta
15	32	64.8	Pasta	15	14	1.13	Household cleaning
16	31	64.1	Shortening, oils	16	34	1.12	Nuts
17	24	63.3	Salad dressings, mayo	17	14	1.10	Breakfast foods
17	14	63.3	Sauces, sauce mixes	17	4	1.10	Fish, canned
17	34	63.3	Syrup	17	13	1.10	Pet foods
20	36	62.5	Dietetic	20	19	1.09	Baking mixes
21	20	60.3	Fruit, canned	20	31	1.09	Fruit, canned
22	36	59.7	Vegetables, dried	20	38	1.09	Salad dressings, mayo
23	8	58.2	Soups	23	26	1.04	Soft drinks
24	33	58.1	Sugar	24	37	1.03	Coffee, tea, cocoa
25	10	57.5	Household cleaning	25	3	.98	Jams, jellies, spreads
26	13	57.1	Prep. foods, canned meats	26	21	.95	Prep. foods, canned meats
27	16	56.9	Cigarettes	26	1	.95	Seasonings, spices
28	14	55.2	Condiments	28	16	.94	Paper products, wraps
29	18	52.7	Baking needs	29	16	.93	Pickles, olives, relish
30	30	51.8	Desserts	30	19	.92	Beverage powders, bases
31	27	50.0	Milk, powdered and canned	30	32	.92	Desserts
32	25	48.6	Baking mixes	30	29	.92	Vegetables, canned
33	29	44.1	Vegetables, canned	33	9	.90	Vegetables
34	19	41.9	Pickles, olives, relish	34	23	.89	Cigarettes
35	28	39.5	Jams, jellies, spreads	35	25	.86	Shortenings, oils
36	38	35.0	Baby foods	36	35	.84	Cookies, crackers
37	35	31.7	Seasonings, spices	37	7	.54	Fruit, dried
38	20	25.0	Fruit, dried	38	5	.40	Sugar

Source: Ibid.

on over 2,000 new products introduced between June 1986 and February 1987. This section presents a statistical description of the product and market characteristics of these products based on both the data furnished by the suppliers and the judgments of the supermarket buyers. The associated acceptance rates are also presented.

Many insights into the nature of new product acceptance can be gained by examining the descriptive statistics of the new products evaluated by our cooperating wholesale-retail firm. Since the firm was selected for its representativeness, we believe most of the statistics reported here may be generalized to other grocery buying organizations.

Tables 4.11 and 4.12 report the mean scores given by the team of six buyers to selected attributes of the new products proposed by manufacturers. The selected attributes are described as follows.

Attribute/Variable	Description
Who Made Presentation (Variable 45)	Depends on whether a broker presented the new product on behalf of a supplier principally (1), whether the supplier's own sales representative made the presentation (2), or whether both were present (3)
Competing Stores (Variable 46)	Indicates how many competing companies in the marketplace already have introduced the new item
Competing Brands (Variable 47)	Indicates how many other branded products in the retail organization are viewed as competing with this new product
Competing Private Label (Variable 48)	Indicates how many other private label products in the retail organization will compete with the new item
Physical Attribute (Variable 49)	Buyer judgment (0–10 scale; 0 = inferior, 10 = superior) on physical performance of item (taste if food product or effectiveness if nonfood)
Package Uniqueness (Variable 50)	Buyer judgment (0–10) on package design and color uniqueness
Vendor Reputation (Variable 51)	Buyer judgment (0–19) of the track record of the supplier based on own or firm's experience
Quality of Presentation (Variable 52)	Buyer judgment (0–10) on the overall quality of the vendor's presentation materials and package
Expected Performance (Variable 53)	Buyer judgment (0–10) on expected growth and performance of the entire product category over the next year
Space Requirements (Variable 54)	Buyer judgment (0–10) on total likely warehouse and store space requirements of item
Profit Contribution (Short Run) (Variable 55)	Buyer judgment (0–10) on short-run total profit contribution potential (during introductory vendor support)
Profit Contribution (Long Run) (Variable 56)	Buyer judgment (0–10) on long-run total profit contribution potential of item (after vendor introductory support is withdrawn)
Advertising/Promotion (Variable 57)	Buyer judgment (0–10) on total vendor advertising and promotional support of item in both short and long runs

Examination of Table 4.11 indicates the substantial differences in buyer evaluation of the various selected attributes as a function of

Table 4.11
Selected Attribute Evaluations by Major Product Category, Mean Scores

Product Category	ATTRIBUTE												
	V45	V46	V47	V48	V49	V50	V51	V52	V53	V54	V55	V56	V57
Baby Foods	1.53	4.54	2.08	0.00	5.36	5.25	6.61	6.42	5.19	2.69	6.53	5.64	3.44
Frozen Foods	2.11	0.85	9.46	0.25	6.93	6.46	6.34	6.39	5.68	4.08	6.92	6.86	4.89
Household Supplies	2.32	0.74	2.94	0.44	6.17	5.88	5.86	5.73	6.10	5.78	6.43	5.74	5.25
Macaroni and Potatoes	2.17	1.89	2.10	0.38	5.54	5.61	5.25	4.48	6.03	6.59	6.53	5.00	4.20
Pet Products	2.49	2.08	4.87	0.67	5.76	5.81	5.83	5.20	6.34	8.77	7.16	5.43	5.22
Sauces, Spices, Etc.	1.83	1.17	3.69	0.31	6.56	6.37	5.70	5.32	6.24	5.31	6.99	5.67	4.94
Snacks, Crackers, Nuts	1.42	0.75	3.05	1.04	4.99	5.04	4.92	4.09	5.58	4.35	6.72	5.38	3.12
Baking Ingredients	1.53	0.44	4.80	1.92	5.00	4.68	4.74	4.16	4.43	3.59	5.53	4.86	2.48
Beverages	1.52	0.62	4.07	2.23	5.76	5.57	5.57	5.34	5.92	5.70	6.21	5.46	3.98
Breads, Cakes	1.44	0.94	10.43	4.66	5.07	5.23	5.10	3.71	4.59	4.41	7.73	6.22	2.06
Breakfast Cereals	1.84	1.50	1.93	0.09	6.12	6.19	6.45	5.72	6.06	5.63	6.50	4.72	4.87
Candy and Gum	1.34	1.43	1.12	0.00	6.47	6.34	5.77	5.48	5.94	5.18	6.40	5.36	3.61
Canned Foods	1.41	0.73	2.81	0.72	5.14	5.27	5.01	4.68	5.47	5.14	6.11	4.97	2.47
Dairy Dept.& Refrig. Food	1.77	0.88	8.10	1.18	6.77	6.37	6.57	6.49	5.85	4.43	7.00	7.10	4.65
Average	1.77	1.33	4.39	0.99	5.83	5.72	5.69	5.23	5.67	5.12	6.63	5.60	3.94

Variables
V45=Who Made Presentation
  1=Broker Only, 2=Manufacturer's Rep. Only, 3=Both
V46=Number of Competing Stores Carrying Item
V47=Number of Competing Items-Brands
V48=Number of Competing Items-Private Label
49-57: 1-10 Range where 0 is most negative and 10 most positive
V49=Physical Attributes
V50=Package
V51=Vendor Reputation
V52=Quality of Vendor Presentation
V53=Expected Performance
V54=Space Requirement
V55=Total Profit Contribution-Short Run
V56=Total Profit Contribution-Long Run
V57=Total Vendor Advertising/Promotion

Source: Cornell Research New Product Evaluation Research Report, Cornell University. (Unpublished). 1990.

product category differences. A marketer of snacks, crackers, and nuts might be concerned, for example, that the physical attributes (Variable 49), presumably taste and perhaps texture to a lesser degree, of this broad product category received only an average buyer rating of 4.99 (out of 10), while other categories are evaluated much more positively; several categories, such as frozen foods and dairy foods, were rated at nearly 7.0. This represents approximately a 40 percent better rating. To an increasing degree, snack food suppliers must compete with other food types for valuable shelf space, so the relatively poor showing for one of the key product attributes should be of concern. Such a finding should send a signal to these companies to conduct further research on the exact nature of this potential problem.

Similarly, bread and cake vendors may have reason to investigate their brokers since two-thirds of all new breads and cakes were presented by brokers, but the buyers rated the quality of the vendor presentation (Variable 52) a 3.7, while dairy and frozen food vendors received approximately 6.5 for their presentations. Buyers are apparently not impressed with the commitment or effectiveness of the vendors of breads and cakes, canned foods, or baking ingredients with respect to total advertising and promotional effort (Variable 57), at least relative to competing categories. These categories received only half as high a rating as, for example, household supplies for the promotional effort. Differences like these should provide individual marketers with the basis for strategy reformulation.

Two additional observations can be made regarding buyers' general orientation. Only two variables evaluated by the buyers had a mean that was not close to 5.0: Short-run profit (Variable 55), which averaged 6.58, and total vendor advertising and promotion evaluation (Variable 57), which averaged only 3.95. In the first instance, this appears to provide cautious corroborative evidence that new products are more profitable at first, or at least buyers perceive them to be. This is likely to be due to both the absence of other products to compete with the new entry, as well as the more lucrative terms generally offered by vendors for the new product's initial entry. In the second case, buyers appear decidedly dissatisfied with the levels of overall promotional and advertising support for new products. Whether this reflects a real opportunity for manufacturers to correct a communication problem perceived by retail buyers or it reflects a time-honored and inevitable conflict between two opposing players in the marketing channel is difficult to determine.

Table 4.12 can be interpreted similarly but serves to recall one important characteristic of supermarket procurement: buying decisions are made by individuals, and individuals differ. Despite procurement guidelines and identical strategies at the corporate level, Table 4.12 am-

Table 4.12
Selected Attribute Evaluations by Individual Buyer, Mean Scores

| Variable/Attribute * | Buyer | | | | | | |
	1	2	3	4	5	6	Mean
1 Who Made Presentation V45	1.57	1.87	1.59	1.52	1.56	1.38	1.53
2 Competing Stores Carrying Item V46	3.07	2.46	1.70	2.93	0.79	1.06	2.17
3 Competing Brands V47	9.08	4.64	4.36	7.88	1.71	2.07	5.78
4 Competing Private Label V48	0.54	0.01	0.62	3.82	0.27	0.23	0.94
5 Physical Attributes V49	6.76	5.58	5.51	5.06	6.08	5.63	5.97
6 Package V50	6.43	5.81	5.82	4.81	6.12	5.76	5.89
7 Vendor Reputation V51	6.38	5.24	5.34	5.03	5.94	5.56	5.75
8 Quality of Presentation V52	6.42	4.83	4.82	3.94	5.91	5.34	5.45
9 Expected Performance V53	5.78	6.41	6.03	5.12	6.21	5.55	5.73
10 Space Requirement V54	4.20	4.58	7.79	3.85	5.12	5.40	5.04
11 Profit Contribution/Short Run V55	6.95	6.65	6.76	6.67	6.59	6.04	6.63
12 Profit Contribution/Long Run V56	6.95	5.98	5.18	5.10	6.15	5.04	5.87
13 Total Vendor Adv./Promotion V57	5.59	5.59	4.83	3.60	5.97	3.33	4.75
Average (Vars. 5-13)	6.16	5.63	5.79	4.80	6.01	5.29	5.67

* Variable 1: 1=Broker Only; 2=Manufacturer's Rep. Only; 3=Both
  Variable 2-4: Range 0-99
  Variable 5-13: Range 0-10

Source: Ibid.

ply shows that strategy gets implemented, insofar as buying decisions
are concerned, in very different ways according to individual buyer
style and personal operating procedures.

Table 4.12 summarizes the individual evaluation of all six buyers on
the retail company's management procurement team with respect to
each of the same variables listed in Table 4.11. Note the significant differences in the averages for all of the individual mean scores among the
buyers. The average total evaluation given to all new products by
Buyer 4 was only 4.8, whereas Buyers 1 and 5 both accorded average
overall ratings to their sets of products of over 6.00. It seems to be clear
that different buyers consistently arrive at very different evaluations,
even when averaging over fairly large samples. To the extent that a
manufacturer can monitor these differences in professional conduct, it
might make good sense, for an individual firm basis with a profit-
maximizing objective, to arrange to present a particular new product to
the buyer(s) with a more generous, or sympathetic, history for product
evaluations. The dilemma with such a strategy, however, is twofold: it
is not always possible to choose the buyer who will be on the receiving
end of any given new product presentation, and, moreover, even if it

were possible, it is not clear that what may or may not be a sound prescription for the individual firm (at least in the short run) would improve performance when this type of strategy is considered from a
systemwide perspective.

After evaluating the many characteristics of each new product, buyers make decisions regarding acceptance or rejection. Tables 4.13 and
4.14 present the buyer acceptance rates for all products, as well as for
key selected subgroups. The overall acceptance rate for the 2,034 products in the sample was 31.9 percent, but the subgroup variation is substantial (Table 4.13). A number of observations are appropriate. First,
some buyers (Buyers 2 and 3) are approximately twice as likely to accept a new product as are other buyers. Whether this is due to individual buyer personality type or the nature of the specific product
category to which the buyer is assigned is a question for future research. Second, the acceptance rates for the various product categories
ranged from 61 percent for pet foods to 11 percent for baby foods.
These differences appear to be independent of the number of items introduced in each category. Third, marketing support is a variable reflecting the proposal of television advertising and/or coupons by the
manufacturer. Support was defined as "none" if neither of these forms
is used by the vendor, "limited" if only one is used, and "high" if both are
offered; in a large number of cases (about 45 percent), this information
was missing. As expected, acceptance rates improved substantially as
vendor's marketing support increased; buyers' likelihood of accepting a
product with television advertising and coupons was nearly twice as
great as in the case where neither of these two promotional vehicles
was present.

We note several trends of interest when examining the acceptance
levels associated with the various other attributes. Acceptance rates
for suggested retail price (SRP) generally increase as price increases,
although the majority of new products are introduced into categories of
price below $1.00 per unit. With the sole exception of the SRP on pro-
motional deal, where acceptance rate decreases once the SRP is greater
than $2.00, this same trend is observed whether the price is the intro-
ductory "deal" price or the "regular" price after the initial price period
has elapsed. The acceptance trends with respect to "deal" and "regular"
gross margin are consistent: they are the highest by a considerable
amount when the product's margin is in the 11 to 20 percent area and
then fall dramatically when gross margin increases beyond 20 percent.
The reason is that the supermarket industry gross margin standard for
dry grocery products falls in this range. While the overall gross margin
average has recently risen to the 24 to 26 percent range, the range for
dry groceries alone is typically closer to 15 to 18 percent.

The number of competing stores (Variable 46) that has already ac-

Table 4.13
Acceptance Rates of New Items Proposed, by Various Criteria

Variable/Category	Number of Items	Acceptance Rate (%)	Variable/Category	Number of Items	Acceptance Rate (%)
Total of All			**Percent Profit (Deal)**		
Products Proposed	2034	31.9	11-20%	462	50.4
			21-30%	607	30.1
Buyers			31%+	965	36.2
1	694	29.7			
2	84	53.6	**Suggested Retail Price (Reg)**		
3	292	48.6	Below $1.00	906	28.7
4	308	23.7	$1.00-2.00	697	31.6
5	162	29.6	$2.00+	431	39.5
6	476	27.9			
			Percent Profit (Reg)		
Product Category			11-20%	707	71.3
Frozen Foods	397	33.0	21-30%	862	32.0
Canned Foods	245	21.2	31%+	465	26.9
Dairy Dept. and Refrigerated Foods	225	28.0			
Beverages	198	28.3	**Number of Competing Stores (V46)**		
Household Supplies	127	29.1	0	1333	29.7
Sauces, Spices, etc.	121	43.8	1	55	27.2
Snacks, Crackers, Nuts	93	25.8	2	134	23.1
Candy and Gum	129	43.4	3	101	36.6
Pet Products	116	61.2	4	84	29.7
Baking Ingredients	84	17.9	5	54	31.5
Breads, Cakes	67	28.4	6	61	44.3
Breakfast Cereals	32	56.3	7	35	28.6
Macaroni and Potatoes	73	31.5	8+	177	51.4
Baby Foods	37	10.8			
			Number of Competing Brands (V47)		
Marketing Support			0	505	36.6
High	528	46.2	1	183	34.4
Limited	114	41.2	2	269	34.6
Low	422	24.4	3	255	23.1
None	970	26.4	4	145	18.6
			5	138	26.1
Suggested Retail Price (Deal)			6 - 9	198	33.8
Below $1.00	1003	27.0	10+	342	35.1
$1.00-2.00	667	35.7			
$2.00+	364	31.9	**Number of Private Label (V48)**		
			0	1500	32.6
			1	343	35.5
			2	63	12.7
			3	55	18.1
			4	14	14.3
			5	25	16.0
			6+	34	41.2

Source: Reprinted from *Journal of Marketing*, Published by the American Marketing Association, Chicago, IL 60606. V. R. Rao and E. W. McLaughlin, "Modeling the Decision to Add New Products by Channel Intermediaries," January 1989, Vol. 53.

Table 4.14
Acceptance Rates of New Items Proposed, by Various Attributes

Score	V49 Proposed		V50		V51		V52	
	#	%	#	%	#	%	#	%
0	79	17.7	7	0.0	2	0.0	41	12.2
1	16	12.5	30	3.3	9	0.0	41	24.4
2	45	0.0	30	6.7	44	20.4	64	17.2
3	79	11.3	70	7.1	114	6.1	94	24.5
4	163	11.6	134	10.4	146	18.5	184	22.3
5	426	20.2	450	17.1	491	27.1	472	25.0
6	524	33.2	598	35.9	496	38.9	542	35.6
7	371	44.2	425	46.1	477	37.7	366	42.1
8	221	54.8	188	51.6	172	47.7	161	44.1
9	84	58.3	43	65.1	11	54.5	15	80.0
10	26	46.2	4	75.0	0	0.0	0	0.0

V45=Who Made Presentation
V46=Number of Competing Stores Carrying Item
V47=Number of Competing Items-Brands
V48=Number of Competing Items-Private Label
V49=Physical Attributes
V50=Package
V51=Vendor Reputation

Source: New Product Evaluation Research Report, Cornell University. (Unpublished).
1990.

cepted the new item appears most often to be 0 according to the results in Table 4.13, but the acceptance rate increases considerably when the number of competing retailers that already have the new product grows above six. Presumably retail buyers are most positively influenced when they see that their peers in other companies have already conducted their own evaluations and have decided to add the product. The variables describing the numbers of competing brands and private labels (Variables 47 and 48) do not display any particular pattern with respect to buyer acceptance.

Table 4.14 shows the number of products and the respective buyer acceptance rate (percentage) for Variables 49–57. As expected, the acceptance rates generally increase as the buyer evaluation of the individual attribute improves from 0 to 10. However, it is equally true that

Table 4.14 (*cont.*)

V53		V54		V55		V56		V57	
#	%	#	%	#	%	#	%	#	%
0	0.0	53	12.0	64	62.5	3	100	143	18.2
7	0.0	26	7.9	1	0.0	4	0.0	125	12.8
23	0.0	64	34.3	8	12.5	23	13.0	160	16.3
145	4.8	226	33.2	21	23.8	54	20.4	235	15.7
176	4.0	413	33.7	37	10.8	188	26.6	193	23.5
462	17.5	668	24.9	294	14.3	537	27.4	355	34.6
573	32.1	291	30.2	545	27.3	514	33.5	298	42.3
384	54.9	114	42.1	632	34.5	427	36.0	214	56.5
164	76.8	68	44.1	288	48.3	191	41.9	89	55.1
33	44.5	36	47.2	100	43.0	30	36.7	58	65.5
5	80.0	75	68.0	44	68.2	4	100	9	66.7

V52=Quality of Vendor Presentation
V53=Expected Performance
V54=Space Requirement
V55=Total Profit Contribution-Short Run
V56=Total Profit Contribution-Long Run
V57=Total Vendor Advertising/Promotion

relatively few products were given a very high (9 or 10) rating on any given attribute; the evaluations for most products fell in the middle range between 4 and 8. One interpretation of this result is that, on average, buyers find the performance of individual attributes for most new products to be average.

Several remarks are appropriate here. First, it should not be surprising that products rated as 0, 1, or 2 were in general not accepted; these acceptance rates were nearly always below 20 percent. Second, in some cases, these low scores, which invariably lead to rejection, could have been avoided. Variable 52, for example, shows the buyer acceptance rates given various levels of the quality of the vendor promotional materials and presentation. Although the comprehensiveness, appropriateness, and professional bearing of these materials and presentation are clearly within the realm of control of the vendor, apparently not enough vendors fully recognize this. Over 20 percent of all products in the study were evaluated by buyers to have a 4 or below on this measure.

Figures 4.1–4.9 summarize certain of the principal statistical results of Tables 4.13 and 4.14. Figure 4.7, for example, points to what many in the grocery trade regard almost as a rule of thumb: when a manufacturer is about to introduce a significantly new product, representatives from the company itself make the presentation, not brokers acting on the behalf of their supplier principal. On such important occasions, they might accompany their normally designated broker to the presentation. This finding does not imply that broker sales forces are not as effective or as professional as manufacturer's own sales representatives; it only draws attention to the fact that the broker must contend with introducing perhaps the less exciting of the new products – those, for example, that may only extend an already-existing line rather than represent a fundamentally new technology.

Figures 4.8 and 4.9 draw attention to a key element of new product introductions: the importance of marketing research and test marketing. The influence of one or both of these attributes appears to have the same general impact on buyer acceptance: it increases it. Buyers are much more likely to accept an item when some form of marketing research is present (43 percent versus 26 percent), and, similarly, buyers accept 40 percent of the products that have test marketing information versus 30 percent when test marketing was not present. In both of these cases, however, note should be taken that the majority of new products today are introduced without either one of these attributes, primarily because of the great increases in the costs of launching a major test marketing or marketing research campaign. However, at the same time, it is evident from Figures 4.8 and 4.9 that when this additional cost is incurred, it has an impact: buyer acceptance rates increase significantly. (The effectiveness of such forms of research in predicting the product's ultimate success in the marketplace is discussed further in Chapter 6.)

Despite the usefulness of much of the information contained in Tables 4.11, 4.12, and 4.13, they all suffer from the irreconcilable inconsistencies often inherent in isolated, raw data when causal relationships in the real world are likely to involve complex interactions and curvilinear relationships. Consider, for example, Table 4.13. Our expectation was that as buyer evaluation approached a "superior" status for each attribute, the buyer(s) would be more likely to accept the product. We see such a monotonic acceptance increase, for example, as buyer's packaging assessment improves. But when examining physical attrib-

Figure 4.1
Percentage of New Products Accepted, by Category

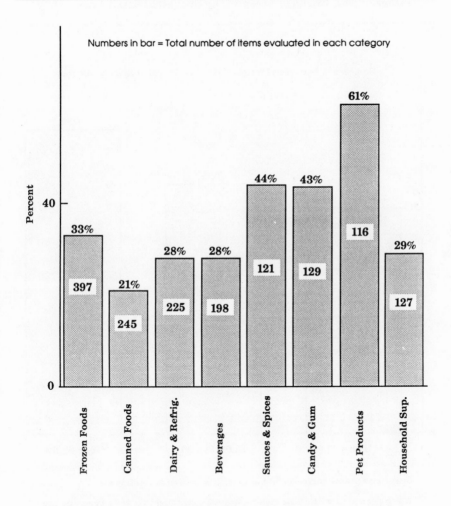

Numbers in bar = Total number of items evaluated in each category

Although acceptance rate for the entire sample of products was 32%, this rate differed significantly by product category

Figure 4.2
Percentage of New Products Accepted, by Suggested Retail Price

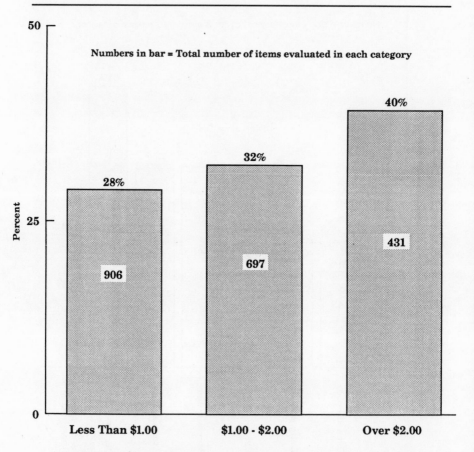

Buyer acceptance increased steadily with increases in retail price

When presented with these results, buyers confirmed that they generally are more favorably disposed to more expensive products

Figure 4.3
Percentage of New Products Accepted, by Marketing Support

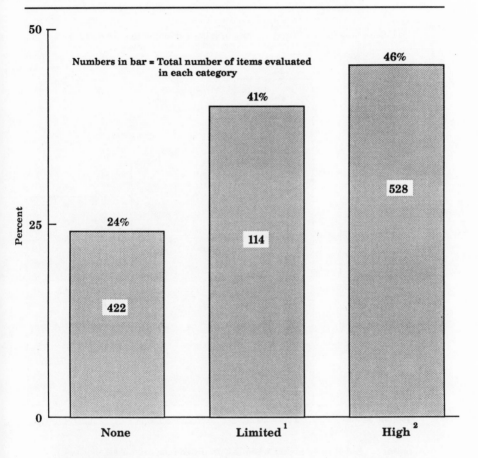

Numbers in bar = Total number of items evaluated
in each category

¹Coupon or T.V.
²Coupon and T.V.

Although information was often missing for many of the marketing support variables, in general, greater marketing support was associated with greater probability of acceptance, as expected.

Figure 4.4
Percentage of New Products Accepted, by Gross Margin

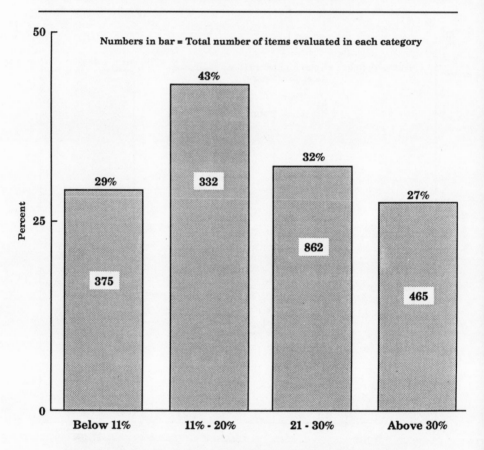

Acceptance tended to be higher when the proposed (non-promotional) gross margin was in the range of the average gross margin for the dry grocery category (ie., 18%-20%).

The lowest acceptance category (28%) was for those products with gross margins over 30%, reflecting perhaps a reluctance to take on products that absorb unusual overhead or handling expenses.

Figure 4.5
Percentage of New Products Accepted, by Vendor Reputation

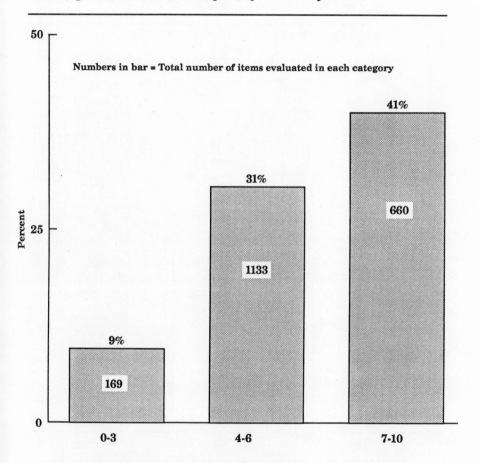

Buyers were asked to evaluate their previous experience with each vendor (eg., vendor reputation) on a 0-10 scale (0 = very negative, 10 = very positive). Although the majority of vendors were rated "average" (4-6), those vendors with the best reputations, not suprisingly, enjoyed the highest acceptance probabilities for their product (40% vs. 10%)

Figure 4.6
Percentage of New Products Accepted, by Presentation Quality

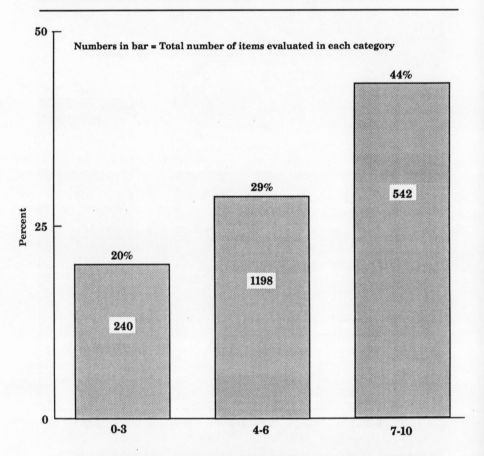

Buyers were asked to evaluate the overall quality of each vendor's presentation on a 0-10 scale (0 = very negative, 10-very positive). Again, although the majority of presentations earned only "average" (4-6), the best presentations (7-10 — tended to produce much higher acceptance rates (44%).

Figure 4.7
Percentage of New Products Accepted, by Presenting Firm Type

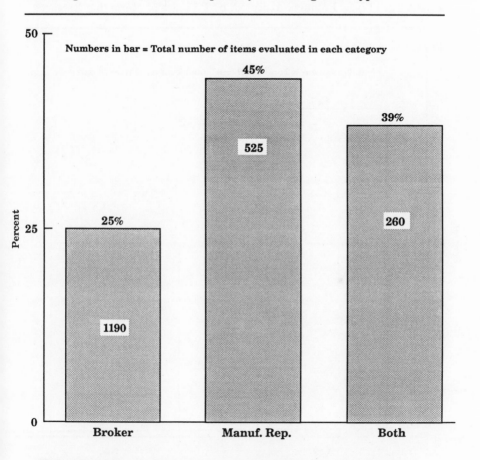

Numbers in bar = Total number of items evaluated in each category

While the majority of all products were presented by brokers, the acceptance rate for these products was only approximately half as high as when a manufacturer's own representative made the presentation.

This may in part be explained by the greater number of re-presentations made by broker sales forces.

Figure 4.8
Percentage of New Products Accepted, by Presence of Marketing Research

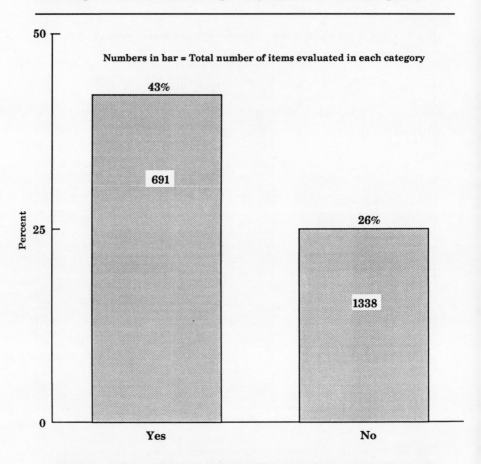

Although nearly two-thirds of all new product presentations were not accompanied by marketing research results, those that were (691 products) tended to be accepted at considerably higher rates (43% vs. 26%).

Figure 4.9
Percentage of New Products Accepted, by Presence of Test Marketing

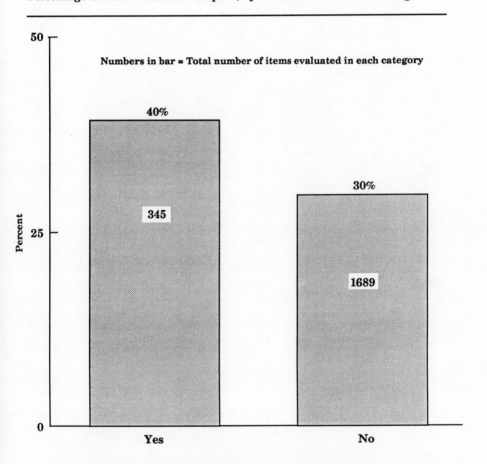

Numbers in bar = Total number of items evaluated in each category

While the great expense of test marketing has dramatically reduced its use, acceptance rates were found to be higher for products presented with test marketing results than those without such data (40% vs. 30%).

ute, a counterintuitive result obtains: over half (53.89 percent) of all products rated a perfect 10 are rejected. Obviously, more analysis of the interactive nature of these variables is required.

5

MODELING ACCEPTANCE AND SUCCESS

This chapter reports the results of the analytical work done to determine the relative importance of various attributes of a new product in the acceptance by trade buyers and success later in the marketplace. We have identified the criteria that could be used in describing the acceptance and success. Essentially, we will consider three evaluative or behavioral variables:

1. Judgments of profit potential from a new product.
2. Decision to recommend acceptance or rejection of the new product.
3. Decision to continue or withdraw the new product.

For convenience, we refer to these as decision variables. The first two of these decision variables are specific to the trade buyer, using the information presented to him or her and inferences drawn from such information. The third variable is specific to the committee based on the sales information since the product is sold in the outlets of the firm. We will use two sets of data: historical data on actual new products and judgmental data on hypothetical new products.

MODELS AND HYPOTHESES

The conceptual model guiding our analysis of the three decision variables regarding a new product by a channel intermediary was presented in Figure 3.1. The buyer, as channel intermediary, operates as an agent for various consumers and evaluates all of the information presented regarding a vendor's new product. Subsequently, the buyer makes a judgment on the overall profit potential for the new product, considering such factors as potential demand for the product and expected costs to the firm, and he or she eventually recommends accepting or rejecting the product. Some of the underlying variables in this assessment are specific to the product and its vendor, and some are specific to the intermediaries. In particular, certain characteristics of the channel intermediary, such as buying committee structure and size of the intermediary firm, can be expected to influence the format and content of the information presented by the vendor or sought by the intermediary. For example, it is likely that when the channel intermediary is a large firm – perhaps a market leader – the information and the manner in which it is presented by the vendor differ from the case when the intermediary is a fringe operator. The number and status of the individuals representing the vendor-manufacturer are likely to differ because the stakes are generally much higher when the new product presentation is made to a large account. Not only is an accepted product likely to mean a larger initial order size, but intermediaries that are market leaders or at least dominant firms have considerable influence over the decisions of the competitors and followers. This appears to be true for buyers' judgments and inferences regarding new products as well as final recommendations.

ACTUAL PRODUCTS

Model for Long-Term Profit Potential Judgment

The long-term profit potential, y, for a new product priced at P and an acquisition cost of C may be written as:

$$y = (P - C)^* \hat{Q}$$

where $\hat{Q}$ is the expected sales quantity. In addition to price alone, buyers' expected sales quantity is determined by a host of marketing variables, including: degree of competition, product characteristics, and vendor support. Gross profit margin is also included. Although it is directly related to price, it is the most widely employed performance criterion in the supermarket industry and has an important influence in forming buyers' perceptions of long-term profit. Additionally, the variable, synergy, is included to capture the influence of existing families of items; it may be relevant particularly for line extensions. Therefore, we can model the long-term profit potential as:

$$y = f(\text{price, profit margin, competition, product characteristics,} \\ \text{vendor support, synergy, other}) \qquad (5.1)$$

This function can be specified as a linear combination of the different variables in the equation. Letting the set of variables on the right-hand side be X, the linear version of this model can be written as:

$$y = \delta + \gamma X + \text{error}$$

where δ is the intercept term and γ is a vector of coefficients showing the impact of the new product attributes on the profit judgment. To ensure comparability across various new products, each variable must be measured on the same scale across products and categories. The data we collected on actual products will enable us to aggregate across various products since the measurement scales are comparable.

Model for Accept or Reject Recommendation

We can specify the functional relationship for the overall evaluation of a new product with defined characteristics X as:

$$\tilde{u}(X) = f(X) + \epsilon \qquad (5.2)$$

where $f(X)$ is the deterministic component of the evaluation dependent on the set of variables X. The term ϵ is the error term (stochastic component) associated with this evaluation. The variables under X can be divided into two groups: Z_1, a set of descriptors for the new product as determined largely by the marketing strategy employed by the vendor, and Z_2, a set of channel intermediary-specific variables. In our empirical study conducted with one channel intermediary, the second set of variables is constant. The variables under the subset Z_1 are those that assist the channel intermediary in the decision regarding whether to add the new product. Effectively, the decision maker makes an evaluation of the likely demand for the new product and the potential profits generated through the various outlets of the channel intermediary firm. Thus, these variables include those that affect the consumer response (demand) and those that affect the intermediary firm's costs.

Under certain assumptions, the functional relationship (5.1) can be transformed into the familiar logistic function:

$$P_j = P[y_j = 1] = \frac{1}{1 + \exp(-\alpha - \beta' x_j)} \qquad (5.3)$$

where:

P_j = probability of acceptance of the jth item by the channel intermediary;

y_j = channel intermediary's decision on jth item (0 for reject; 1 for accept);

$\underset{\sim}{x_j}$ = (px1) vector of descriptors measured for the jth item;

$\underset{\sim}{\beta}$ = (px1) vector of parameters;

α = an intercept term.

Model for Continuation Decision

New product attributes play a significant role in the marketplace performance of the product. Assuming that a product's performance is a predominant factor in the continuation decision, the model relating to the decision to continue will be quite similar to that of the decision to accept or reject the product, however, the coefficients associated with each attribute will be different. Naturally, the universe of products on which this model will be based is much smaller than that for the accept-reject decision.

Variables and Hypotheses

In Table 5.1, we have grouped these variables into four categories: financial, competition, marketing strategy, and other. Classified under the market strategy category, we defined four so-called terms of trade variables. These four factors were selected on the basis of average frequency of appearance in the new product presentation package and on a factor analysis performed on a larger group of nonprice incentives offered by certain vendors originally consisting of the following nine variables: slotting allowances, off-invoice terms, bill-back provisions, display allowances, early buy plans, deal minimum order quantity, free cases, additional promotional deal periods, and special advertising funds. The highest average frequency of appearance were off-invoice (present in 59 percent of all new product presentations), free cases (present in 26 percent of all new product presentations), slotting allowances (present in 13 percent of all new product presentations), and bill-back provisions (present in 11 percent of all new product presentations). The results of the factor analysis confirmed that the four factors we chose preserve the majority of the information furnished by the complete set of nine variables, while reducing the redundancy and making the modeling and interpretation more manageable.

Further, we have hypothesized the direction of influence of each variable on the three decision variables: profit judgment, the decision to accept a new product, and the decision to continue. Since we anticipate that these new product attributes operate in a similar manner with re-

Table 5.1
Variables and Hypotheses for Actual New Products

Category	Variable	Hypothesized Direction of Influence on the Accept/Reject Recommendation+
FINANCIAL	Gross Margin	Positive (?)
	Profit per unit shelf space	Positive (?)
	Opportunity cost of capital needed to obtain the new item	Negative
COMPETITION	Number of firms in the trading area	Positive (?)
	Number of competing brands	Negative
MARKETING STRATEGY	Product uniqueness	Positive
	Vendor effort	Positive
	Marketing support	Positive
	Terms of trade	Positive or Negative
	Price	Positive (?)
OTHER	Category growth	Positive
	Synergy with existing items	Negative (?)

+These hypotheses are same for the profit potential and the continuation decision.

gard to the three decision variables, we will focus our discussion on the critical decision of accepting or rejecting the new product.

Financial Variables. Both gross margin and unit profit are hypothesized to have a positive influence on the decision to accept a new product because of their presumed association with net profitability. These measures – gross margin particularly – are the most frequently employed indexes of profitability in the wholesale-retail grocery industry and, thus, irrespective of their lack of complete congruence with net profitability, generally behave as if the terms could be used interchangeably. However, in reality, these relationships are complex and far from monotonic. For example, a high gross profit may imply a high net profit, but a gross profit is typically determined by subtracting vendor cost from the retail price, which in nearly 90 percent of the cases is

established by both the normal range of the category and by the manufacturer's suggested retail price (SRP). Although it is certainly within
his or her control to do so, in fact, it is rare that a retailer decides not to
use the vendor SRP. Therefore, it is likely that a vendor establishes a
relatively high SRP, and thus correspondingly high gross margin, because of the recognition that the particular product requires additional
retailer costs, such as with products that need extra handling or bulky
products that occupy valuable space. In these cases, even though the
gross profit may be high, the additional marginal costs to the
wholesaler-retailer may result in a final net profit that is in fact low.
Hence, our hypothesized positive relationships among gross profit,
unit profit, and buyer acceptance are felt to be weak.

We expect the relationship between the decision to take on a new
product and an approximate measure of opportunity cost to be negative. Here we employ the minimum number of cases required from vendors for an order times the cost per case as a proxy for the amount of
capital needed to "invest" in the new product. This approach can be
thought of as the opportunity cost and approximate measure of risk or
alternatively, commitment, in the new product as a result of the natural
reluctance by retailers to tie up their resources in the inventory of the
new product.

Second, two competition variables are hypothesized as having opposite impacts: number of competing firms and number of competing
brands. First, buyers' decisions to add new products were hypothesized
as being positively influenced by the number of competing firms in the
trading area already carrying that product. This positive association
derives from buyers' practice of closely monitoring new product additions of competitors; specifically, the greater the number of these competitors that have already positively evaluated a new product, the
greater is the likelihood that a buyer will also add the product. However, the number of competing or substitute brands (national brands
and private label), given space constraints in both warehouse and store,
is hypothesized to influence negatively the likelihood of acceptance.

Marketing Strategy. We expect positive relationships between the
intermediary's decision to accept a new product and the marketing
strategy variables under the control of the vendor: product uniqueness
(e.g., distinctive aspects of new product's quality and packaging), vendor advertising and promotion, nonprice term of trade, and price. Product uniqueness and vendor's advertising and promotion will directly
influence ultimate consumer demand for the new product and hence are
likely to have positive impacts on the intermediary's decision. The nonprice terms of trade will generally have a positive impact on the accept
decision; however, certain nonprice terms of trade (e.g., bill back) are
perceived to be less beneficial by the intermediary due to the high

transactional effort involved. Finally, the directional impact of the price variable is hard to predict. While higher prices will dampen the movement of goods at the consumer level, they are also likely to be associated with higher gross profit. In the former case, the impact of price is expected to be negative, and in the latter case, positive.

Other. New items in fast-growing product categories are expected to be accepted with higher probabilities by channel intermediaries. A new item's synergy with existing products is hypothesized to influence acceptance probability negatively. The reasoning here was based on physical space limitation; intermediaries are less likely to add line extensions to existing families of products.

Estimation Methods. The profit variable is measured on an interval scale (0–10), while the other two decision variables are binary (yes or no). The technique of ordinary least squares (multiple regression) is appropriate for estimating the effects of new product variables on the profit judgment but not for the other two dependent variables. Their models are the logistic regression models and are estimated by maximum likelihood methods. The LOGIST procedure developed by Walker and Duncan (1967) and implemented in the SAS package (Harrell, 1985) is suitable for this purpose and utilized here.

Impact Measures. The marginal impact of the kth attribute of a new product on the decision variable of profit is measured by the regression coefficient, γ_k in the model. However, the marginal impact of the kth predictor variable in the models of acceptance or continuation decision is measured by the equation

$$\frac{\partial P_j}{\partial x_k} = \beta_k P_j (1 - P_j) \tag{5.4}$$

where P_j is the probability of accepting the jth new product in the acceptance model (or the probability of continuing with the jth new product in the continuation model). Unlike the ordinary multiple regression of profit judgment on the X variables, the measure shown in equation 5.4 is not constant; it increases (decreases) as the acceptance probability varies from 0 to 1 if β_k is positive (negative). Thus, the impact measure depends on the values of the other predictor variables that contribute to the probability of acceptance. This property of the measure suggests that interactive effects of the several predictor variables are implicitly included in the model.

HYPOTHETICAL NEW PRODUCTS

Two measures – judgment of long-term profit potential and recommendation for acceptance or rejection – were provided for each profile of a hypothetical new product. The profit potential was evaluated on a five-point scale, while the recommendation was a binary scaled (yes/no) measure. In a manner similar to the actual products, the method of multiple regression was used for estimating the model of profit potential, and logistic regression was employed for the model of recommendation. These data enable us to look for correspondence among the various criteria employed between actual and hypothetical products. Noting that each attribute of the hypothetical new product was described as a profile using different levels, the analyses were done after converting each attribute into a number of dummy variables (one less than the number of levels). In that sense, these models are quite akin to conjoint models reported in the marketing research literature with increasing frequency. In fact, Wittink and Cattin (1989) documented 200 conjoint commercial analyses a year between 1981 and 1985 and concluded that it is likely that since 1985, the use of conjoint applications may be even more widespread due primarily to increased familiarization of researchers and the availability of commercial software to perform the analyses.

Conjoint analysis offers a way to decompose the individual buyer's evaluation of a profile of hypothetical products into various components, each component specific to product attributes included in the profile. The basic premise of our application of conjoint analysis is that in viewing the new items as multiattributed alternatives, we can separate out the functions associated with the influence of the attributes of each vendor's marketing strategy. These attribute-specific functions are called "part-worth" functions. The normalized range of the attribute-specific part-worth function will indicate the relative importance of each attribute.

This method allows us to make predictions about future buyer choice behavior. One obvious extension of this method of analysis is that product designers and marketers can use the results to answer questions regarding the best combination of attributes to build into a new product and its marketing strategy to ensure both buyer and marketplace acceptance.

Various hypotheses can be developed—in a manner similar to that for actual products—on the way each attribute will influence the recommendation decision or the judgment of profit potential. These are shown in Table 5.2.

MODELS FOR PROFIT JUDGMENTS

Actual Products

In the case of actual products presented to buyers, we have elicited evaluation of buyers on the long-term profit potential (under the condi-

Table 5.2
Variables and Hypotheses for Hypothetical New Products

Category	Variable	Hypothesized Direction of Influence on the Accept/Reject Recommendation+
FINANCIAL	Percent gross profit margin	Positive
	Additional introductory market development funds	Positive (?)
COMPETITION	Number of firms in the trading area	Positive (?)
	Number of competing brands	Negative
MARKETING STRATEGY	Product uniqueness	Positive
	Product status	Positive or Negative
	Vendor effort (test marketing; presentation and p-o-p materials)	Positive
	Marketing support (TV advertising, coupons)	Positive
	Price	Positive
OTHER	Category growth	Positive
	Price experience with vendor	Positive

+These hypotheses are same for the judgment of profit potential.

tions of normal vendor support after the withdrawal of introductory support). A 0–10 scale was used. The results are presented in Table 5.3.

The overall fit of this model is quite high (with an adjusted R^2 of 0.43) and is statistically significant. This model is developed for all observations in various product categories, using dummy variables for eight categories. Their use was intended to include any variability among the product categories. As one would expect, many of the product category effects are important. Four of the variables – gross margin, vendor effort, one terms-of-trade variable, and expected category growth – show statistically significant effects. These are according to the hypotheses discussed. It is rather surprising that the variables measuring the competition (both firms and brands) are not significant.

Among the four terms-of-trade variables included in the model (as dummy variables), only the presence or absence of bill-back provision is

Table 5.3
Results of Multiple Regression of Long-Term and Short-Term Profit Potential Judgments

Variable	Long-term Profit Potential		Short-term Profit Potential	
	Regression Coefficient	t-value	Regression Coefficient	t-value
Intercept	2.91	12.74	4.73	18.05
Gross Margin	0.049	9.74	0.006	1.05
Profit Per Shelf Volume	−0.87E-3	−1.06	−0.92E-3	−1.00
Opportunity Cost	0.26E-5	1.07	−0.38*E-5	−1.36
Number of Competing Firms	−0.009	−0.70	0.016	1.08
Number of Competing Brands	0.004	0.64	−0.004	−0.50
Product Uniqueness	−0.02	−1.08	0.04	2.16
Vendor Effort	0.08	4.89	0.04	2.41
Terms of Trade Dummies				
Off-invoice	−0.10	−1.41	−0.04	−0.49
Slotting allowance	−0.18	−1.89	0.08	0.75
Bill back	0.21	2.07	0.12	1.05
Free cases	−0.06	−0.81	−0.03	−0.33
Low Price Dummy	−0.19	−1.98	0.30	2.79
Medium Price Dummy	−0.09	−1.06	−0.02	−0.25
Expected Category Growth	0.15	5.98	0.13	4.42
Synergy Dummy	0.10	1.41	0.21	2.71
Product Category Dummies		(See below)		
Number of Observations	1017		1023	
Adjusted R-Square	0.43		0.13	
F-Ratio	34.40		7.61	
D.F.	23,993		23,999	
P-value	0.0001		0.0001	

Product Category	Long-term Profit Potential		Short-term Profit Potential	
	Estimate of Effect*	t-value	Estimate of Effect*	t-value
Frozen Foods	1.18	10.66	0.24	1.89
Canned Foods	0.02	0.16	−0.40	−3.10
Dairy Foods	1.11	8.76	0.02	0.12
Beverages	−0.27	−1.60	−0.35	−1.84
Household Supplies	0.44	2.98	−0.12	−0.71
Sauces, Spices, etc.	0.41	2.62	0.02	0.10
Candy & Gum	−0.35	−2.35	−0.32	−1.91
Snacks, Crackers, etc.	−0.24	−1.49	0.13	0.71
Other	0		0	

*Relative to "other" category.

statistically significant; the effect is positive. Surprisingly, the offer of a slotting allowance shows a negative effect on the long-term profit potential judgment, perhaps because of the assessment that the offer of slotting allowances is made only one time in the initial period of introduction of the product. Furthermore, buyers responded that the result regarding this seemingly inconsistent finding was indeed predictable. In fact, they explained, slotting allowances are offered, or at least increased, only when the vendors suspect that inherent product quality is weak. Buyers, recognizing this tactic, may reject products with larger-than-normal slotting allowances since these monies serve as a cue for poor quality. Conversely, products that are clearly unique and of demonstrable superior quality are easily recognizable to buyers and are accepted on their own merits, without the aid of slotting allowances.

The effects of the price variable, although not significant, are in the expected direction: low-priced products are judged to generate lower profit potential.

The dummy variable for synergy with existing products is not significant, but the sign of the effect is positive in the expected direction.

Relative to all other categories, new products belonging to frozen foods and dairy foods are judged to offer higher profit potential in the long term. This result has considerable face validity in the light of probable changing demand structures. During the period of data collection for this study, the expansion of premium frozen foods was changing consumer perceptions of the quality of the frozen foods category, and both consumer demand and retail freezer space grew as a result. The category of candy and gum is deemed to offer much lower profit potential in the long run.

Hypothetical Products

The judgments of likely profit potential are related to various attributes of the hypothetical products using multiple regression. The results are presented in Table 5.4, where each block shows the part-worth function for the corresponding attribute. The ranges of these part-worth functions can be used to indicate the importance of the attributes. Profit margins, for example, has the greatest range between the lowest and the highest part-worth function. The normalized ranges, shown below in descending order, indicate that two critical attributes are gross margin and number of competing brands. In addition, there are differences among the buyers (which are due to product categories). The part-worth functions for the two most important attributes are presented in Figure 5.1.

The graphs in Figure 5.1 can be employed to estimate how a change in the level of any specific attribute will affect the overall profit poten-

Table 5.4

Part-Worth Functions for Various Attributes of Hypothetical New Products Based on Profit Potential Judgments Using Multiple Regression Analysis

Attribute and Level	Part-worth Function	Attribute and Level	Part-worth Function
PROFIT MARGIN		PRODUCT STATUS	
Much below average	0	Entirely new product	-0.02
Below average	0.17	Me-too product	-0.05
Average	0.15	Line extension of size	-0.09
Above average	0.47	Line extension of pack	-0.03
Much above average	0.55	Line extension of formulation	0
PRIOR EXPERIENCE WITH VENDOR		NUMBER OF COMPETING FIRMS	
Highly unfavorable	0	Zero	0
Unfavorable	-0.02	One	-0.07
Neutral (no experience)	0.08	Three	0.01
Favorable	0.03	Six	-0.05
Highly favorable	0.13	Eight	-0.01
PRODUCT UNIQUENESS		NUMBER OF COMPETING BRANDS	
Much inferior	0	Zero	0
Below average	0.08	One	0.48
Average	0.07	Three	0.31
Above average	0.13	Six	0.16
Outstanding	0.18	Eight	0.11
SUGGESTED RETAIL PRICE		TV ADVERTISING SUPPORT	
Much below average	0	Much inferior	0
Below average	-0.02	Below average	0.05
About average	-0.07	About average	0.07
Above average	0.08	Above average	0.04
Much above average	-0.06	Outstanding	-0.11

tial evaluation of buyers. That is, we see that if a manufacturer increased the profit margin from the "average" level to the "much above average" level, the normalized buyer evaluation would increase from approximately .16 to .55. Moreover, the part-worth functions here allow measurements to be made regarding the trade-offs possible between levels of attributes. The following list, for example, shows that the total profit potential evaluation of buyers will remain about the same even if profit margin is decreased from "much above average" to "below average" (about a .25 reduction), as long as the product is introduced into a company or market (or even category) that has only two competing brands instead of, say, six or seven (in this case, about a .25 *increase*):

Table 5.4 (cont.)

Attribute and Level	Part-worth Function	Attribute and Level	Part-worth Function
COUPONS SUPPORT		DUMMY VARIABLES FOR BUYERS	
Not utilized	0	Buyer 1	0
Much inferior	-0.07	Buyer 2	0.41
Below average	-0.04	Buyer 3	0.34
Above average	0.08	Buyer 4	0.41
Outstanding	-0.07	Buyer 5	0.46
TEST MARKET/M.R. RESULTS		STATISTICS OF FIT	
Not provided	0	Adjusted R-Square	0.07
Not convincing	0.07	F-Ratio	2.26
Moderately convincing	0.06	D.F.	51,74
High convincing	0.05		9
PRESENTATION AND P-O-P MATERIALS			
Not available	0		
Much inferior quality	-0.03		
Low quality	-0.03		
High quality	-0.11		
Outstanding	-0.12		
INTRODUCTORY MARKET DEVELOPMENT FUNDS			
Not available	0		
Much inferior	-0.14		
Below average	-0.03		
Above average	-0.13		
Outstanding	-0.14		

Attribute	Measure of Importance
Gross Profit Margin	20%
Number of Competing Brands	18
Buyers	17
Product Uniqueness	6
TV Support	6
Coupons	6
Retail Price	6
Introductory Market Development Funds	5
Point-of-Purchase Materials	4
Prior Experience with Vendor	4

Figure 5.1
**Part-Worth Functions of Profit Potential for Two Important Attributes:
Hypothetical Products**

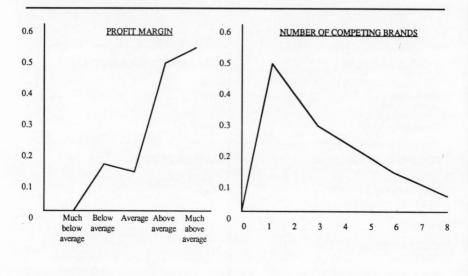

Product Status	3
Number of Competing Firms	3
Test Market Results	2

Gross Profit Margin. This function is according to expectations. The gross profit margins at above-average and much-above-average levels are judged to yield higher profit potential.

Number of Competing Brands. As one would expect, the function shows a negative slope with increasing number of brands competing with the new product under evaluation. There is, however, a premium in not being the only brand in the category, as indicated by the lowest value for "zero" level of this attribute.

Buyer. Buyers differ in their overall profit judgments. These differences are due to the particular product categories associated with each buyer. That is, the different buyers were responsible for different product categories, each characterized by attributes with different importance weights.

Product Uniqueness. This function is in the expected direction; the range is small, indicating relative lack of importance.

Television Advertising Support. This attribute is not very important in the evaluation of profit potential, but buyers seem to value moderate to above average levels more than outstanding levels. It is likely that excessive (outstanding) advertising is deemed by buyers to result in fewer funds available to vendors to support the trade in other ways (e.g., in-store promotions) and therefore a lower judgment of profit potential.

Coupon Support. According to this part-worth function, likely profit is at its optimum when there is above-average support of coupons by vendor. Either too much or too little coupon support is judged to yield lower profit potential. Outstanding coupon levels can often be viewed as negative by retailers if they employ double-coupon programs because they pay out to shoppers the same amount as on the manufacturer coupon. The participating retailer in this study had such a program. In fact, "not utilizing" coupons is judged more valuable than levels other than "above average."

Retail Price. This function shows very small effects of various levels of retail price. It appears that more expensive products are judged to yield lower profit potential. This is undoubtedly related to turnover. Buyers must assume from experience that high-priced products are often likely to be slow moving and thus yield low profit dollars, irrespective of what may be a high per-unit profit.

Introductory Market Development Funds. It is hard to interpret the function for this attribute. It appears that buyers show some skepticism when vendors offer additional funds under this rubric to motivate the buyer to accept their new product.

Point-of-Purchase Materials. This attribute does not carry any weight in the evaluations of profit potential.

Prior Experience with Vendor. Although the range for the part-worth function of this attribute is small, there is a positive effect on profit judgment for vendors with favorable experience and a negative effect on profit judgment for unfavorable experience.

Product Status. It is rather surprising that buyers valued the status of the new product minimally. The (lack of) range here indicates an attribute of little importance.

Number of Competing Firms. There is some premium in being the first firm to reap any profit potential, but this attribute shows a minimal effect; the range of the part-worth function is too small.

Test Market Results. Buyers do not place any value on this attribute in their evaluations of profit potential.

MODELS FOR ACCEPTANCE

Actual Products

The acceptance or rejection decision model was estimated using logistic regression. The data were divided randomly into two subsamples for analysis and validation; the validation data constituted about one-third of the total sample. The major analysis consisted of building logistic regression models for all categories of items, for subgroups of items with several levels of marketing support and for groups of items of different price ranges. Analyses for subgroups of items were conducted to account for the inherent heterogeneity among the various categories of products.

The estimated coefficients for the variables for the model are shown in Table 5.5. As shown, the model chi-square is highly significant. Further, the coefficients of the majority of the variables are in the predicted direction. The variables of product uniqueness, expected category growth, and number of competing firms show positive and significant effects. The variable bill-back terms of trade show negative and significant effects. These results are according to our hypotheses. That is, in the case of the positive variables, we expected that a new product that was evaluated by the buyers as unique, in a category where high growth was expected, and where the number of competing firms that had already accepted the product was high would itself be evaluated high and be likely to be accepted. Conversely, for the negative variable, the bill-back provision is a nonprice terms-of-trade factor that is apparently regarded by buyers as creating higher transactions costs than it is worth in extra revenue. Hence, when evaluated in conjunction with the generally positive terms-of-trade variables, bill-back provisions actually have a negative overall impact on buyers' likelihood to accept the product.

The only variable with a negative and significant effect is gross margin, for which we hypothesized a weak positive relationship. This finding is consistent with results of Montgomery (1973), however, who found that the relationship between new product acceptance and gross margin was negative but not significant. The only other variables that appear with a contradictory sign were the remaining terms-of-trade factors, but their coefficients are not statistically significant.

Product Category Effects. The effects of the product categories are estimated by the use of dummy variables in the logistical model. The estimated coefficients for the overall model presented in Table 5.6 show that the acceptance probability differs significantly across the product categories. The more negative the coefficient is for a category, the lower is the probability of acceptance of an item in that category, relative to a comparable item in the Others category. Illustrative acceptance probabilities are shown in Table 5.6 assuming .4 is the acceptance probability in the Others category; naturally these probabilities will change with changes in the reference probability of the Others category. Relative to an item in the Others category, the chances of being accepted are lower for comparable item profiles in frozen foods, dairy foods, beverages, and household supplies, and they are higher for candy and gum. Other

Table 5.5
Estimated Logistic Model for Acceptance or Rejection of Actual
New Products

Variable	Coefficient (chi-square)@
Intercept	−5.47 (41.92) *
Gross Margin	−0.06 (10.30) *
Profit Per Shelf Volume	0.004 (3.24) +
Opportunity Cost	−0.001 (1.14) +
Number of Competing Firms	0.14 (11.72) *+
Number of Competing Brands	−0.03 (1.89) +
Quality Measure	0.25 (18.03) *+
Vendor Effort	0.03 (0.46) +
Expected Category Growth	0.68 (46.49) *+
Synergy Dummy	−0.31 (2.01) +
Terms of Trade Dummies:	
Off-Invoice	−0.19 (0.70)
Slotting Allowance	−0.43 (2.03)
Bill Back	−0.93 (6.04) *
Free Cases	−0.22 (0.87)
Low Price Dummy	−0.17 (0.30)
Medium Price Dummy	0.02 (0.01)
Product Category Dummies	(Shown in Table 5.6)
Number of Observations	687
Model Chi-Square, D.F.	249.49; 23
P-Value	0.0

@The chi-square is with 1 degree of freedom.
*Significant at 0.05 level.
+Sign according to expectations.

Source: E. W. McLaughlin and V. R. Rao, "The Strategic Role of Supermarket Buyer Intermediaries in New Product Selection: Implications for Systemwide Efficiency," *American Journal of Agricultural Economics* 72 (May 1990).

Table 5.6
Product Category Specific Effects in the Overall Logistic Model of Acceptance or Rejection

Major Product Categories	Coefficient for Dummy Variable[a]	Illustrative Acceptance Probabilities for Comparable Items[+]
Frozen Foods	−1.17 (10.24)*	0.171
Canned Foods	−0.63 (3.33)	0.262
Dairy and Refrigerated Foods	−1.51 (13.52)*	0.128
Beverages	−1.36 (5.86)*	0.146
Household Supplies	−1.94 (15.27)*	0.087
Sauces, Spices, etc.	−0.85 (3.38)	0.222
Candy & Gum	0.26 (0.38)	0.464
Snacks, Crackers, & Nuts	−0.91 (2.26)	0.212
Others	0	0.4

*Significant at the 5 percent level.
[a]The numbers in parentheses are chi-square values for each coefficient (with 1 d.f.).
+These were computed for items with identical characteristics using a base of 0.4 probability for Others category.

Source: Reprinted from *Journal of Marketing,* Published by the American Marketing Association, Chicago, IL 60606. V. R. Rao and E. W. McLaughlin, "Modeling the Decision to Add New Products by Channel Intermediaries," January 1989, Vol. 53.

Table 5.7
Predictive Validation Using the Overall Model

Actual Decision	Model's Prediction		Total
	Reject	Accept	
Accept	196	29	225
Reject	65	48	113
Total	261	77	338

differences are not statistically significant. The reasons for these differences are likely to be found in the relative lack of merchandising appeal
despite large gross margins (household supplies), the constraints of
space (dominant for frozen and refrigerated foods), and apparent lack of
significant brand differences among selected product categories (e.g.,
beverages and dairy department items).

Model Fit and Validation.

Actual	Prediction		Total
	Accept	Reject	
Accept	125	98	223
Reject	51	413	464
Total	176	511	687

The percentage of total correct predictions or the classification accuracy $(125 + 413) \div 687 = 78.6$ percent is very high; this accuracy is
much higher than that of a random model that yields a hit rate of $\alpha^2 +$
$(1 - \alpha)^2$ where α is the prior probability of acceptance. Using the observed acceptance rate of 0.32 as an estimate of α, the classification
accuracy for the random model is approximately 56 percent. Examining the other statistics of the fit – percentage correct accept or sensitivity (56.5 percent) and percentage correct reject or specificity (89.2
percent) – we find that the logistic model predicts the reject decision
much better than the accept decision. This result is perhaps due to our
model's inability to capture all of the idiosyncratic factors associated
with the accept decision.

In order to obtain more insight on the workings of the model, it is
validated using the validation subsample. The results of validation,
shown in Table 5.7, are impressive: the overall model correctly predicts
over 72 percent of decisions.

Given the large number of items (sixty-five) rejected according to the
fitted model but accepted by the intermediary, we probed further into
the actual decision process. For this purpose, a sample of twenty-seven
of these items was presented to the buyers to elaborate on the reasons
for their accept decisions. Interestingly, the buyers were able to recall
vividly the circumstances surrounding the introduction of each of the
items. The reasons expressed for their initial acceptance and the status
of the items after approximately two years are summarized as follows:

Reasons for Acceptance

Low price: fourteen items

Product uniqueness: seven items

Completion of line: two items

Other: four items

Status after Twelve Months

Discontinued: six items

Likely to be discontinued: four items

Selling well: eleven items

Selling quite well: six items

In our discussion, buyers indicated that five of the fourteen items accepted for reasons primarily of low price were accepted for temporary distribution only. Further, three of the seven items accepted for product uniqueness reasons, were taken on to satisfy the specialized demands of several local ethnic groups. Moreover, ten of the twenty-seven items were either discontinued or likely to be discontinued shortly. Therefore, there seem to be special characteristics associated with items accepted by buyers but predicted as rejects by the model.

We can use the observed rate of discontinuance of the items – ten of twenty-seven items – in revising the predictive power of our model. A table showing the revised accept and reject decisions follows:

Actual Decisions	Model's Prediction		Total
	Accept	Reject	
Accept	165	58	223
Reject	51	413	464
Total	216	471	687

Accordingly, the hit rate improves to $(165 + 413)/687 = 84$ percent. Incorporation of such revised data will enable researchers to develop better predictions of new product acceptance.

Model Structure for Subgroups. The logistic model was also estimated for subgroups of items – by marketing support and by price. The statistics on fit of these models are presented in Table 5.8. As could be expected, the classification accuracy improves for the various subgroups of items (due to greater homogeneity within a subgroup). The classification accuracy – percentage of correct predictions – ranges from 78.6 percent to over 90.3 percent.

Explanations of the coefficient estimates (not presented here) of the subgroup models revealed a few differences. First, for the "highly supported" items, opportunity cost of capital and price dummies are significant with negative signs, results that could be expected. Second, for

Table 5.8
Classification Accuracy of Logistic Models for Accept and Reject Decisions

Model for	Number of Items	Number Accepted	percent Correct Hits
All Items	687	223	78.6
Unsupported Items	194	85	83.5
Highly Supported Items	155	41	90.3
Low-Priced Items	237	68	80.2
Medium-Priced Items	289	98	81.3
High-Priced Items	161	57	88.8

Source: Reprinted from *Journal of Marketing,* Published by the American Marketing Association, Chicago, IL 60606. V. R. Rao and E. W. McLaughlin, "Modeling the Decision to Add New Products by Channel Intermediaries," January 1989, Vol. 53.

low-priced items, as the intensity of vendor effort and profit per shelf volume increase, the probability of acceptance increases. These differences suggest that in-depth analyses of the variation inherent in subgroups might be a fruitful area for future research.

Hypothetical Products

Logistic regression was employed to estimate the relationship between the response of recommending acceptance or rejection of the hypothetical new product and its attributes. Various product category differences are included by a set of dummy variables; since each group of categories was evaluated by a buyer, these variables were essentially coded as four dummy variables for the five buyers. The results are presented in Table 5.9. The estimated beta coefficients are presented as part-worth functions for the different attributes.

Using the range of the values of the part-worth function, a measure of relative importance of each attribute is derived. In descending order of importance, the attributes stack up as follows:

Table 5.9
Part-Worth Functions for Various Attributes of Hypothetical New Products Based on Accept-Reject Recommendation Using Logistic Regression Analysis

Attribute and Level	Part-worth Function*	Attribute and Level	Part-worth Function*
PROFIT MARGIN		PRODUCT STATUS	
Much below average	0	Entirely new product	0.07 (0.06)
Below average	0.09 (0.09)	Me-too product	0.19 (0.46)
Average	0.27 (0.82)	Line extension of size	-0.003 (0)
Above average	0.71 (5.91)	Line extension of pack	0.16 (0.32)
Much above average	0.71 (6.13)	Line extension of formulation	0
PRIOR EXPERIENCE WITH VENDOR		NUMBER OF COMPETING FIRMS	
		Zero	0
Highly unfavorable	0	One	-0.13 (0.20)
Unfavorable	1.14 (14.48)	Three	0.28 (0.88)
Neutral (no experience)	1.48 (22.03)	Six	0.05 (0.04)
Favorable	0.97 (10.74)	Eight	-0.25 (0.73)
Highly favorable	0.50 (2.69)		
PRODUCT UNIQUENESS		NUMBER OF COMPETING BRANDS	
Much inferior	0	Zero	0
Below average	0.66 (5.15)	One	0.69 (5.65)
Average	0.06 (0.04)	Three	0.22 (0.59)
Above average	0.22 (0.53)	Six	-0.14 (0.21)
Outstanding	0.48 (2.53)	Eight	0.11 (0.13)
SUGGESTED RETAIL PRICE		TV ADVERTISING SUPPORT	
Much below average	0	Much inferior	0
Below average	0.10 (0.13)	Below average	-0.58 (0.04)
About average	0.02 (0.01)	About average	0.22 (0.62)
Above average	-0.30 (1.08)	Above average	-0.24 (0.67)
Much above average	-0.39 (1.77)	Outstanding	-0.29 (0.91)

*Numbers in parentheses are corresponding chi-square values.

Table 5.9 *(cont.)*

Attribute and Level	Part-worth Function*	Attribute and Level	Part-worth Function*
COUPONS SUPPORT		DUMMY VARIABLES FOR BUYERS	
Not utilized	0	Buyer 1	0
Much inferior	0.36 (1.58)	Buyer 2	2.82 (66.64)
Below average	0.12 (0.15)	Buyer 3	2.15 (41.58)
Above average	0.42 (2.20)	Buyer 4	2.12 (38.91)
Outstanding	-0.18 (0.38)	Buyer 5	0.66 (3.13)
TEST MARKET/M.R. RESULTS		INTERCEPT	
Not provided	0	Alpha 1	-3.81 (28.45)
Not convincing	-0.08 (0.09)		
Moderately convincing	-0.02 (0.01)		
High convincing	0.31 (1.15)		
PRESENTATION AND P-O-P MATERIALS		STATISTICS OF FIT	
		Adjusted R-Square	170.22
Not available	0	D.F.	51
Much inferior quality	-0.38 (1.58)		
Low quality	-0.39 (1.86)		
High quality	-0.27 (1.01)		
Outstanding	-0.37 (1.56)		
INTRODUCTORY MARKET DEVELOPMENT FUNDS			
Not available	0		
Much inferior	-0.11 (0.16)		
Below average	-0.39 (1.89)		
Above average	-0.36 (1.44)		
Outstanding	-0.50 (2.93)		

*Numbers in parentheses are corresponding chi-square values.

Attribute	Measure of Importance
Buyer	26 percent
Prior experience with vendor	14
Number of competing brands	8
Television advertising support	8
Product uniqueness	6
Coupon support	6
Number of competing firms	5
Introductory market development funds	5
Suggested retail price	5
Test market/market research results	4
Presentation and point-of-purchase materials	4
Product status	2

It is quite clear that the accept recommendation is very much influenced by the product category in question (or by the buyer evaluating it). The next most important attributes of the new product that influence the accept recommendation are prior experience with the vendor, number of competing brands, and degree of television advertising support offered by the vendor. The remaining attributes, in order of decreasing importance, are: product uniqueness, coupon support, number of competing firms, extent of introductory market development funds, suggested retail price, test market/market research results, presentation and point-of-purchase materials, and product status. It is quite interesting to note the low importance accorded to the product status as implied by these judgments.

While the analysis reveals a few anomalies in some part-worth functions, it is of interest to discuss each of them. For illustrative purposes, the part-worth functions for the two most important attributes (other than product category) are shown in Figure 5.2.

Buyer. There are substantial differences in the different buyers (note the highly significant chi-square statistic), which we assume are related to the heterogeneous product categories to which the buyers are assigned.

Prior Experience with Vendor. The part-worth function for this attribute is anomalous on the face of it since buyers seem to indicate the highest effect for "neutral" experience and decreasing effects for experiences that are either more or less favorable. In a way, this function shows a certain degree of objectivity on the part of the buyers; there does not seem to be a penalty for prior unfavorable experience or additional consideration accorded to vendors with highly favorable experience.

Figure 5.2
Part-Worth Functions for Selected New Product Attributes for the Decision to Recommend

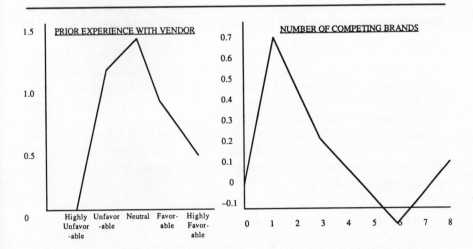

Number of Competing Brands. As in the case of competing firms, buyers seem to accept new products that have limited competition inside the chain. At the same time, they seem to be reluctant to be the first in the market.

Television Advertising Support. The part-worth function for this variable shows that buyers do not prefer products that are either too highly supported by television advertising or too poorly supported. About average levels are sufficient to derive maximum effect of this attribute.

Product Uniqueness. Buyers seem to prefer products that are either outstanding (extremely new) or below average. In general, the probability of acceptance increases with better scores on product uniqueness.

Coupon Support. Products that do not offer coupon support or those that offer just above average level seem to be preferred by buyers. Too much coupon activity is undoubtedly deemed as a detriment for gaining acceptance by the buyers.

Number of Competing Firms. There is a tendency among buyers not to be the first or one of the last in trying out a new product. They want some evidence of market acceptance before accepting a new product on their own.

Introductory Market Development Funds. The estimated part-worth function shows clearly that provision of these funds is not conducive to gain acceptance.

Suggested Retail Price. There is an increasing tendency to shy away from products priced much above average in each product category.

Test Market/Market Research Results. Any results of test market and market research should be highly convincing to have any effect. In general, this attribute is minimal in its impact on the acceptance decision.

Presentation and Point-of-Purchase Materials. While this attribute does not carry much weight, it is unclear what the best level for it should be to gain acceptance. The estimated part-worth function shows results contrary to expectations; however, the part-worth functions are not significant in any case.

Product Status. While there may be a correlation between this attribute and that of product uniqueness, "me-too" products seem to be preferred by the buyers. This result is inconsistent with nearly all industry experience.

COMPARISON OF THE ANALYSES

When comparing the conjoint analyses of the various attributes of our hypothetical products based on buyers' profit potential judgments with that base on actual acceptance-rejection recommendations, several similarities are evident. Certain of the attributes emerged as important in their function in determining profit potential as well as in determining the ultimate acceptance-rejection decision. This is to be expected since, as we hypothesized, profit potential should be positively correlated to the accept-reject recommendation. In fact, five of the six attributes are the same in both analyses when ranked by the most important part-worth functions. In both cases, gross profit margin is one of the key attributes and exhibits a positive slope; that is, higher levels of gross profit are associated with higher levels of profit potential and acceptance. Similarly, there exist substantial differences among the buyers in predicting profit potential and acceptance. These differences are thought to be associated with the heterogeneity of the product categories they evaluate. Moreover, the television support, coupon support, product uniqueness, and number of competing brands all behaved in approximately the same way and emerged as key attributes. The part-worth function of the last variable, for example, exhibited nearly identical properties in both analyses.

It is puzzling, however, that certain of the other attributes that we had expected to behave similarly in both models in fact did not. We hypothesized, for example, that prior experience with the vendor would be an important determinant in explaining evaluation of profit potential as it was in determining the accept-reject decision, but it was not. It is possible that buyers are able to use a vendor's track record as a good indicator of acceptance, whereas they are apparently less certain of the impact of that track record for profit potential.

VARIABLES AFFECTING DECISION TO CONTINUE WITH A NEW PRODUCT

To understand better the relationship of the buyer as the channel intermediary between the manufacturer and the consumer (or marketplace), additional data were collected from the participating retail firm on the status of the subset of all products accepted from the original set of products presented by vendors. Table 5.10 reports the status for these 549 products (29 percent of the original sample). Of the 549 accepted products, 31.9 percent (175 products), or 9.2 percent of the original sample presented, were still on the retail shelves, selling well nearly two years after the initial vendor presentation. Although 69.1 percent of the products initially accepted by the buying organization were discontinued within the first two years, buyers reported a variety of reasons for this deletion decision. The three categories buyers most often cited were lack of consumer interest (45.3 percent of all deletions), expiration of manufacturer introductory allowances (12.9 percent), and the introduction of a superior competing item (11.5 percent).

Table 5.10 also shows the profile of attributes present in the set of products initially accepted by the buying committee as compared to the profile of attributes (variables) of the products that ultimately were accepted by consumers (or by the market) after two years. These comparisons show numerous differences among the attributes present in the group of products accepted by the buyer-intermediaries (buyer acceptance) and the group of products ultimately accepted by the marketplace (consumer acceptance).

The last column in Table 5.10 is an index of the approximate efficiency with which the buying committee was able to predict consumer acceptance computed as the ratio of percentage of products accepted by the buying committee and the percentage of products "accepted" by consumers in the marketplace after two years. Thus, this ratio is an approximate measure of the degree to which the buying committee (in the role of an agent for consumers) and consumers evaluate new products in an equivalent manner. A score of 1.00 indicates that buyers were able to anticipate consumers' final judgment perfectly with respect to the importance of the selected attribute. An index greater (less) than 1.00 suggests that buyers "overestimated" ("underestimated") the importance of an attribute, at least as determined by the proportion of all the products ultimately accepted by the marketplace that exhibit this attribute. For example, of all products accepted by the buying committee, 21.7 percent had test market results presented to

Table 5.10

Profiles of New Products Accepted by Buying Committee versus Accepted by Consumers (Marketplace), Two Years after Introduction, by Major Attribute

Variable/Attribute	Products Introduced Total	Buying Committee Acceptance	Consumer (Market) Acceptance	Index of Buying Committee Acceptance to Consumer Acceptance
Number of Products	1899	549 (29.0percent)	175 (31.9percent)	0.91
Test Market Results Presented	322	21.7percent	28.0percent	0.78
Market Research Data Presented	642	46.3	46.3	1.00
Terms of Trade				
Slotting Allowances Offered	258	14.2	10.3	1.38
Off-Invoice Allowance Offered	1186	68.5	70.3	0.97
Free Cases Offered	501	27.9	30.9	0.90
Bill Back Provisions	204	8.9	10.9	0.82
Financial				
Profit/C.ft. <= $3.00	1218	56.1	61.1	0.92
Profit/C.ft. > $3.00	681	43.9	38.9	1.13
Opp. Cost < $1,000	1101	64.3	65.7	0.98
Opp. Cost $1000-$10,000	596	25.1	20.0	1.26
Opp. Cost > $10,000	202	10.6	14.3	0.74
Gross Margin < 14%	403	18.8	20.0	0.94
Gross Margin 14% - 24%	441	27.9	27.4	1.02
Gross Margin > 24%	1054	53.4	52.6	1.02
Product Characteristics				
Uniqueness <= 12	1159	39.0	36.6	1.07
Uniqueness 13-14	449	32.6	40.6	0.80
Uniqueness >= 15	291	28.4	22.9	1.24
Vendor Effort <= 10	1039	35.3	34.9	1.01
Vendor Effort 11-13	604	37.5	35.4	1.06
Vendor Effort >= 14	256	27.1	29.7	0.91
Retail Price < $1	830	36.8	39.4	0.93
Retail Price $1-$2	648	33.5	37.7	0.89
Retail Price > $2	421	29.7	22.9	1.30
Categ. Growth <= 5	848	17.5	14.3	1.22
Categ. Growth >= 6	1051	82.5	85.7	0.96
Synergy (Related to existing products)	1071	50.8	52.0	0.98

Table 5.10 (*cont.*)

Variable/Attribute	Products Introduced Total	Buying Committee Acceptance	Consumer (Market) Acceptance	Index of Buying Committee Acceptance to Consumer Acceptance
Competition				
# Competing Firms = 0	984	50.5	45.7	1.10
# Competing Firms = 1-6	367	18.9	21.7	0.87
# Competing Firms > 6	547	30.6	32.6	0.94
# Competing Brands = 0	975	58.7	57.1	1.03
# Competing Brands > 5	924	41.4	42.9	0.96
Product Categories:				
Frozen Foods	385	22.5	26.4	0.85
Canned Foods	241	8.2	8.1	1.02
Dairy Foods	207	8.2	10.3	0.80
Beverages	184	8.2	4.0	2.05
Household Supplies	110	4.6	8.1	0.57
Sauces, Spices, etc.	104	7.1	5.8	1.24
Candy & Gum	116	9.5	5.2	1.84
Snacks, Crackers, etc.	87	3.3	4.0	0.82
Other	700	28.3	28.2	1.01

Source: E. W. McLaughlin and V. R. Rao, "The Strategic Role of Supermarket Buyer Intermediaries in New Product Selection: Implications for Systemwide Efficiency," *American Journal of Agricultural Economics* 72 (May 1990).

buyers as part of the vendors' new product presentation; however, 28.0 percent of the successful products (those still on shelves after two years) were those that had had such test market results originally presented. The resulting index, .78, suggests that buyers underestimated the importance of test market results in determining ultimate marketplace success.

The attributes for which the index is either very large or very small are shown in Figure 5.3. For example, products given high scores on product uniqueness by buyers do not necessarily gain consumer acceptance to the same degree (the index is 1.24, showing the possible inefficiency of the buying committee to predict consumer acceptance). In other words, buyers apparently overestimate the importance of this attribute. This is true to a still greater degree with the product categories candy and gum and beverages. This phenomenon can probably be explained by some set of circumstances unique to these two categories at the time of the study; perhaps it was a period of intense, especially convincing advertising by the suppliers.

Figure 5.3
Index of Relative Factor Importance, Buyer versus Consumer

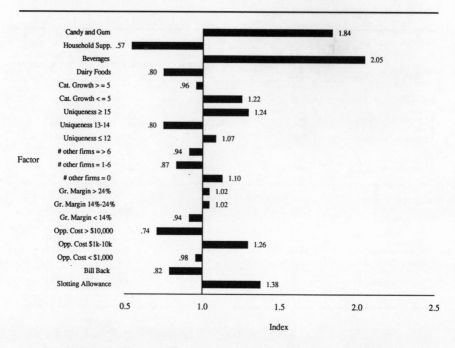

Source: E. W. McLaughlin and V. R. Rao, "The Strategic Role of Supermarket Buyer Intermediaries in New Product Selection: Implications for Systemwide Efficiency," *American Journal of Agricultural Economics* 72 (May 1990).

Indeed, it is interesting to note that our analysis shows that buyers overestimate the importance of slotting allowance, at least as judged by consumers two years later. This finding reinforces our logistic regression findings, as well as much conventional wisdom in the grocery trade: slotting allowances are more readily available for inferior products that are not likely to withstand the test of the marketplace on their own merits. Thus, consumers did not "vote" for products possessing slotting allowance provisions to anywhere near the same levels that buyers did. Despite consumer skepticism, buyer acceptance of such otherwise "inferior" products that came equipped with a slotting allowance may still be a rational economic decision for the retail firm, since the additional revenues gained from a lucrative slotting allowance may more than outweigh the opportunity cost of having a suboptimal product taking up valuable shelf space. Such conjecture requires more research.

SUMMARY AND IMPLICATIONS

This chapter reported on the modeling of the accept-reject decisions by one channel intermediary for new items. Generally the statistical results are significant, and the explanatory variables behaved as predicted. Such analysis should prove useful to manufacturers in the new product development process, especially in marketing budget allocation decisions. Grocery product marketers are regularly forced to make resource allocation decisions with little information regarding the probabilities of likely outcomes. Operating under limited budgets, a marketing manager of a packaged goods firm might need information regarding the expected payoff for additional investment in marketing effort, say, couponing or television advertising, for a proposed new product or to extending the line or family of an existing product or category. The analysis here suggests that the appropriate response to such a question depends on the product's price. Specifically, there is a positive nonsignificant impact on buyer acceptance when a low-price item (under $1.00) is evaluated as part of a family; the opposite result seems to hold when the item is priced over $1.00 (medium price), and there is a significant negative effect for items over $2.00 (high price).

Our analysis clearly points out that different categories of products are evaluated by buyers differently. Manufacturers need to identify and recognize these differences when they develop new product introduction strategies.

The lack of significant positive effects of certain terms of trade (e.g., slotting allowance and free cases) and, indeed, the significant negative effect of others (e.g., bill-back provisions) have several implications for total food system efficiency. Although this result appears contrary to certain of the conduct model's prior expectations and contrary to much popular industry perception, a possible hypothesis is that the presence of certain nonprice incentives, such as slotting allowances, may be correlated with inferior products. That is, suppliers may offer additional support for products they fear are not truly unique, and buyers may recognize and accept truly superior products on their own merits, without additional inducements. In fact, when the buyers in the participating retail firm were confronted with this initially puzzling result, they corroborated that the hypothesis is accurate. Moreover, the attribute profile of products that had withstood the test of the marketplace — those selling well after two years — suggests that buyers apparently "overestimated" the importance of the slotting allowances (the index was 1.38). This finding also suggests that buyers may initially accept products that are accompanied by slotting allowances, perhaps due to the financial incentive alone, only to discontinue them relatively sooner than competing new items without allowances.

Finally, our data show that a higher percentage of products were accepted when market research results were presented (39 percent of products with test marketing or marketing research results were accepted versus 28 percent acceptance rate for products without these results). As a result, one could suggest that, given the high costs of test marketing a new item with consumers, manufacturers instead simply introduce the item to the buyer first. The buyer frequently is in a better position than a manufacturer to assess potential consumer demand. Thus, this procedure may serve as a quick and inexpensive market test. In this sense, recent large numbers of new product introductions may not represent inefficient product proliferation but an efficient manufacturer strategy to increase variety (and profit) while reducing systemwide costs.

6

APPLICATIONS OF ACCEPTANCE MODELS

The preceding chapters covered the topics of developing statistical models to describe the accept-reject decision and the continue-withdraw decisions for a new product by a retail organization. These models were developed using the data on decisions on actual new products and judgments on hypothetical new products collected from buyers in a large retail organization. The work reported thus far indicates that the buyers' decision process can be systematized; their decision-making tasks can be made simpler with a system that utilizes various pieces of data provided by vendors in a statistical model.

Although the models showed a high degree of face validity and described decisions and judgments quite well, they did not fully capture the decision process. This result indicates that certain aspects of expertise of buyers were not incorporated into the statistical models. Thus, it seems logical to suggest that buyers' expertise on certain issues will need to be integrated more fully with the statistical modeling to yield a greater degree of predictive power.

One way to accomplish this integration of statistical models and buyers' expertise not captured by the models is to develop an integrative decision support system or an expert system. A retail organization can develop an expert system, which may be called BUYACXPERT for short, by following several of the currently existing ways of building such expert systems. Liebowitz (1990) describes the similarities and differences among decision support systems and expert systems, ways in which they can be built, and how they are interdependent on each other. This chapter will describe some main ideas for building an expert system and its potential uses. Although this expert system will be described from the perspective of a retail organization, it can also be used by manufacturers. By performing a what-if analysis, manufacturers will be able to determine which strategic variables of the new product should be altered and by how much in order to gain higher levels of acceptance by trade. Such a system will augment currently existing new product pretest market models, which deal with the distribution's role only in a cursory manner.

A BASIC DECISION SUPPORT SYSTEM

The statistical models (based on logistic regression) for new product acceptance can be directly implemented by a retail organization. The organization must: develop instruments for collecting judgmental data of the kind we used in the previous chapter, collect necessary data and build up a database of historical data on new products and decisions, estimate the logistic regression model, and use the estimated model for predicting the probability of acceptance for a new product.

A rule can be developed to reach a decision using this estimated probability; for example, if the probability of acceptance is very high (0.6), accept the product, if it is very low (below 0.2) reject the product, and if it is between, bring the product decision to the attention of the buying committee. In the last situation, the committee may seek more information before deciding or simply make a decision with the data available. Such a simple procedure can immensely reduce the workload of the buying committee and consequently, make the retail firm procurement system more efficient. A flowchart of this procedure is shown in Figure 6.1. Effectively, the buyer assimilates and makes inferences about the new product and examines the levels of the variables that (our) theory and (his or her) experience have shown are important influences on, perhaps determinants of, acceptance and marketplace success. Much of the drudgery and risk may be removed from this process with the aid of an expert system, BUYACXPERT, or New Prodsim. This model essentially provides the coefficient weights developed by our modeling efforts and applies them in a statistical routine to the new variable levels as presented by the vendor. Given an estimate of probability of acceptance and, given some decision rule like the one suggested above, an accept/reject recommendation is determined. At this point, the buyers and/or buying committee may wish to modify or override the expert system recommendation as a function of their experience, particular marketplace conditions, or other relevant information not captured in the formal model. Finally, an actual recommendation decision is made. As new products are evaluated, the data can be updated and the model reestimated. Updating will enable the parameters of the model to be current and in accord with the judgmental processes adopted by the committee and the buyers.

Figure 6.1
Computation of the Initial Decision by a Buyer to Accept a New Product

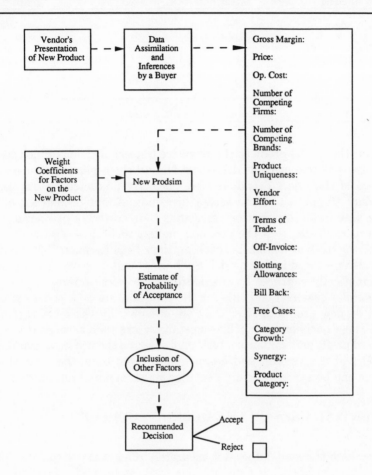

In order to examine the reasons for using an expert system, we have computed the probability of acceptance for twenty-four new products, three each in eight product categories, using the logistic model reported in Table 5.1. The results are shown in Table 6.1. An examination of the last two columns — estimated probability of acceptance and actual decision — reveals that the model has missed a number of times in both directions (accept and reject). Using the decision rule described, the committee decisions on these twenty-four products compare with the predicted decisions as shown in the following diagram.

Predicted Decision	Actual Decision		Total
	Accept	Reject	
Accept	3	1	4
May seek more information	2	3	5
Reject	5	10	15
Total	10	14	24

In fact, the model predicts the negative (reject) decisions much better than the positive (accept) decisions. Ninety-three percent (fourteen of fifteen) of the reject decisions were correctly predicted by our model but only 40 percent of the accept decisions. About 36 percent of the "may seek more information" decisions were correctly predicted. This analysis indicates that the decision makers include several additional factors or rules of thumb in reaching their final decision that we have not fully captured in our model. Such judgmental factors can be more systematically captured by considering an expert system.

A similar case can be made for the continuation or withdrawal decisions on new products after they are accepted by the retail organization. These decisions will utilize a set of factors such as sales trend and realized profit and some variables that describe the product, marketing support of the vendor, and competition. Even here, the expertise of buyers can be systematically captured by an expert system.

POTENTIAL USES OF THE DECISION SUPPORT SYSTEM

Although the model does not accurately predict the actual decisions a high percentage of the time, various uses can be made of the decision model for acceptance described in the previous section. In order to examine this, we have reestimated the acceptance probability under certain changed conditions for four of the twenty-four products shown in Table 6.1. We evaluated changes that may be implemented by the vendor (e.g., product uniqueness) or those that could be bargained by the buyer (e.g., vendor effort or terms of trade). In either case, the costs for implementing these changes will almost invariably be borne by the manufacturer. Changes in product uniqueness call for additional developmental work to improve the product, whereas other changes assume that product quality is unaltered.

For each of these products, certain changes were made in the offer terms and conditions of the new product. The results, presented in Table 6.2, suggest that the manufacturer can utilize the model of acceptance with some advantage. For example, the vendor of Abbott's of New England Smoked Salmon may have gained trade acceptance by removing the established constraints on minimum order quantity (originally set at the equivalent of a \$2,430 investment in new product), bringing the opportunity cost of capital for the trade to zero. Moreover, Abbott's might have invested in additional vendor effort, resulting, say, in moving the vendor effort evaluation from 5.5 to 7.5. In the case of the Wishbone's Blended Italian Dressing, however, improvements in product uniqueness and vendor effort do not seem to matter; the trade accepted this product, but our estimate of acceptance probability is effectively zero. The computations for Delmonte Blended Juice Drinks indicate that the vendor may have made an appropriate offer to gain the trade acceptance initially. In fact, the addition of the seemingly positive terms-of-trade variables, bill-back provisions and free cases, has the perverse result of lowering acceptance probability substantially. Because the impact of these variables is generally negative, this result should not be surprising.

TOWARD A NEW PRODUCT ACCEPTANCE EXPERT SYSTEM

The accumulation of knowledge and expertise in a specialized field like new product evaluations requires decades and careers of human experience. Yet most retail organizations discard this knowledge by allowing the individuals responsible for new product management to retire or move onward without documenting and retaining their acquired expertise. Our attempt here is to recover some of that knowledge in a systematic way through an expert system.

Decisions on new product acceptance and continuance are made quite frequently by retail organizations. Various heuristics (rules of thumb) are employed in reaching them. The knowledge of these heuristics is essentially resident with the buyers. Such a knowledge is generally lost if a buyer leaves the organization. The tools of developing an expert system are ideally suited to systematizing this knowledge and to maintaining a sense of consistency of decisions over time and across different individuals. In our conceptualization, the statistical models we have developed can be augmented by these heuristics.

A retail organization can develop an expert system for new product accept-reject and continuation decisions by a retail organization in order to achieve one or more of the following goals:

- Reaching the accept-reject decision for a new product offered to the retailer
- Identifying variables in the vendor's offer (such as terms of trade) that require improvement in order to gain acceptance

Table 6.1
Comparison of Actual Decisions versus Computed Probabilities of Acceptance for Selected New Products

New Product	Product Category	Gross Margin (%)	Profit Per 1 c. ft. Shelf Volume ($)	Opportunity Cost * 10^3 ($)	Number of Competing Firms	Number of Competing Brands	Product Uniqueness*
Microwave Tater Tots	Frozen Foods	8	1.92	1.12	5	1	7.0
Delicaseas Crab Medlee	Frozen Foods	6	4.90	2.64	2	1	4.5
Ore-Ida Vegetable Crop	Frozen Foods	7	4.63	11.70	0	2	7.0
Seneca Cranberry Juice Cocktail	Canned Foods	5	2.33	5.10	0	6	6.5
Morzano Tomato Puree	Canned Foods	5	5.11	9.60	0	4	5
Delmonte Blend Juice Drinks - Pineapple and Mandarin	Canned Foods	5	7.07	0.51	6	6	6
Pillsbury Buttermilk Biscuits	Dairy and Refrigerated Foods	7	0.70	3.30	5	10	7.5
American Whipped Dips - King Avacado	Dairy and Refrigerated Foods	7	0.11	0.69	3	15	6
Frigo Snack Cheese Swiss	Dairy and Refrigerated Foods	9	1.06	0.97	0	0	7.5
Purified Drinking Water	Beverages	2	2.16	0	0	2	3.5
Wyler's Iced Tea with Lemon	Beverages	5	3.19	9.60	0	10	3
Nescafe Mountain Blend Decaf	Beverages	5	5.15	6.33	0	4	6
Renuizit Roommate - Cool Breeze	Household Supplies	6	1.76	0.38	3	2	6.5
Renuizit Roommate	Household Supplies	7	1.76	0.38	3	1	7
Dispoer Care	Household Supplies	6	1.38	0.91	0	0	6
Wishbone Blended Italian Dressing	Sauces, Spices, etc.	6	0.82	18.7	0	1	6.5
Bama Mayonese	Sauces, Spices, etc.	5	0.84	13.2	0	0	5
Abbott's of New England Smoked Salmon	Sauces, Spices, etc.	7	1.56	2.43	0	4	9
Rascals Fruit Family Bag	Candy & Gum	7	0.05	0.11	0	1	7.5
Chocolate Peanut Clusters	Candy & Gum	5	5.22	1.8	0	3	6
Trident 8's Floor Stand	Candy & Gum	5	22.42	0.64	0	3	5
Sierra Trail Mix - Fruit Snack	Snacks, Crackers & Nuts	5	2.13	1.14	0	2	6
Cashew Halves	Snacks, Crackers & Nuts	4	6.98	18.9	0	6	3.5
Cherry Fruit Snacks	Snacks, Crackers & Nuts	7	2.22	3.59	0	1	5.5

*Measured on a 1 (low) to 10 (high) scale; actual scores in the model were twice these values.

+Low: Under $1.00; medium: $1.00–2.00 and high: over $2.00 per unit.

Table 6.1 (cont.)

	Terms of Trade							Estimated Probability of Acceptance	
Vendor Effort[a]	Slotting Allowances	Off-Invoice	Bill Back	Free Cases	Price Category[+]	Category Growth[a]	Product Synergy		Actual Decision
7.5	No	No	No	Yes	Low	6	Yes	0.44	Yes
5.0	Yes	No	Yes	No	High	3	Yes	0.002	No
6.5	Yes	No	No	Yes	Medium	7	No	0.000	Yes
4.5	Yes	No	No	Yes	High	6	Yes	0.008	No
3	No	No	No	No	Low	5	Yes	0.000	No
5.5	Yes	Yes	No	No	High	6	No	0.64	Yes
6.5	Yes	No	No	No	Low	7	Yes	0.11	Yes
7	Yes	No	No	Yes	Low	7	Yes	0.30	No
6.5	Yes	No	No	No	Low	9	No	0.81	No
3	No	No	No	No	Low	4	No	0.07	No
2.5	No	No	No	No	Medium	4	Yes	0.000	No
5	No	No	No	Yes	High	6	No	0.002	Yes
6	No	No	No	No	Medium	6	Yes	0.41	No
6.5	Yes	No	No	Yes	Medium	7	No	0.61	Yes
5.5	Yes	No	No	No	Medium	7	Yes	0.32	Yes
6.5	No	No	No	No	Low	7	No	0.000	Yes
4	No	No	No	No	Medium	6	Yes	0.000	No
5.5	No	No	No	Yes	Medium	6	Yes	0.29	No
4.5	Yes	No	Yes	No	Medium	7	No	0.87	Yes
3	Yes	No	No	No	High	5	Yes	0.21	No
5	Yes	No	Yes	No	Medium	5	No	0.26	No
5.5	No	Yes	Yes	No	Medium	6	Yes	0.11	No
2	Yes	No	No	No	High	7	No	0.0000	No
2.5	No	No	No	No	Medium	7	Yes	0.05	Yes

Table 6.2
Illustrative Computations of Acceptance Probabilities for Selected Changes
in Vendor Offers for Four New Products

New Products and Committee's Decision	Variable(s) Changed in the Offer	Value of the Variable		Probability of Acceptance	
		Current	New	Current	New
Delmonte Blended Juice Drinks-- Pineapple and Mandarin	Product Uniqueness	6	7.5	0.64	0.79
(Accepted by the committee)	Vendor Effort	5.5	7.5	0.64	0.67
	Vendor Effort	5.5	7.5	0.64	0.38
	Terms of Trade: Bill back Free cases	No No	Yes Yes		
	Product Uniqueness	6	7.5	0.64	0.57
	Vendor Effort	5.5	7.5		
	Terms of Trade: Bill back Free cases	No No	Yes Yes		
Renuizit Roommate -- Cool Breeze	Product Uniqueness	6.5	7.5	0.41	0.53
(Rejected by the committee)	Vendor Effort	5.5	7.5	0.41	0.43
Abbott's of New England Smoked Salmon	Vendor Effort	5.5	7.5	0.29	0.84
(Rejected by the committee)	Opportunity Cost of Capital (* $000s)	2.43	0		
Wishbone Blended Italian Dressing	Product Uniqueness	6.5	9.0	0.000	0.000
(Accepted by the committee)	Vendor Effort	6.5	8.0		

- Filling out the details of a partial new product specification (in order to gain acceptance)
- Reaching the continue-withdraw decision for an accepted new product

Of course, a manufacturer can develop its own expert system (or employ someone else's model) to arrive at the answers for many of the same questions posed from the perspective of the manufacturer. Similar to various expert systems, the buyer acceptance expert system could be developed using any of the commercially available shells of expert systems, such as GURU, KNOWLEDGE WORKBENCH, and RULEMASTER (see, for example, Turban, 1988). Using the terminology of expert systems, the proposed system will consist of three main components: a dialog structure, an inference engine, and a knowledge base. The dialog structure serves as the language interface through which the user accesses the system, usually in an interactive mode. The inference engine component of the system is a computer program that allows hypotheses on the relationships between new product characteristics and acceptance-rejection or continuance-withdrawal of a new product. Based on the accumulated information in the knowledge base, these relationships are derived both statistically and with the deployment of search methods. The search methods will utilize information on both accepted and rejected products and identify some rules buyers use in making the decisions. They may even utilize information not included in the statistical models. These methods are of three types: backward chaining, forward chaining, and forward and backward processing combined. In fact, it is in this search process that the statistical models described earlier in the book can be augmented by rules derived by other means and various hypotheses are developed. The third component of knowledge base is the most important component of the system. The statistical models of acceptance (or continuation) will become part of the knowledge base and will be updated as new data on decisions are entered into the system. The buyer's set of facts and heuristics also will be part of this knowledge base.

SOME DETAILS OF THE SYSTEM

Database

We propose that the lowest-level data be represented as relational data tables, constructed, queried, modified, and maintained by SQL (Structured Query Language) commands (van der Lans, 1989). This is a widely supported ANSI-ISO standard, and, for that reason alone, it is a sensible choice.

Using the research reported earlier, we suggest that the primary data be collected using two questionnaires, one completed by the trade buyer and the other by the vendor. The trade buyer form asks for ratings along a ten-point scale, where 1 or 2 is low, 5 is average, and 9 or 10 is high. The vendor form is of the fill-in-the-blank style where the answers provided are of different dimensions and measure types; these are chosen to be the conventional way of reporting whichever data-value is being elicited. Table 6.3 illustrates the details of such data.

The database will be called The Product Decisions Data Base. It will contain the data gathered in the two questionnaires and the two decisions of accept-reject and continue-withdraw. The database will be augmented with special data tables to allow a greater depth and freedom to the information that it holds. Examples of such tables are shown in Figure 6.2.

Knowledge Base

Estimation of Probabilities. Once the tables are created, filled, and updated as needed, they can be used to estimate the probability information: the probability of acceptance and the probability of rejection over the entire database of brand offerings of various descriptions. Also, these probabilities can be used as prior probabilities when evaluating the likelihood of acceptance of some new brand. Other probabilities can also be derived from the information base—for example, when a new brand has been rated and it is desired to know the likelihood of acceptance or rejection for a brand with characteristics "at least as good as this new brand."

Logistic regression can be used as an information manipulation method leading to knowledge that can then be added to the knowledge base. An illustration of this part of the knowledge base is shown in Figure 6.3 using three independent variables: Performance, Packaging, and Reputation. An option can be provided in the system to isolate those variables that are statistically significant and to conduct various sensitivity analyses of the kind shown in the figure.

In addition, the knowledge base will accumulate various heuristics. This step involves not only various search procedures but also asking the buyers to provide their implicit rules of thumb. As and when exceptions to the predicted decisions based on the statistical model are made, there will be a clear opportunity to add to the stock of these rules. When various rules are in conflict (they lead to opposite decisions), there is a need to resolve them. Effective strategies for this resolution will be part of the knowledge base.

The development of an expert system is typically evolutionary and

Table 6.3
Detail of Data in the Product Decisions Database

A. Supplied by the Trade Buyer

Description	Abbreviation	Type
1) The Item Under Consideration	Item_Name	String
2) Channel Intermediary	Buyer	String
3) Competitors Carrying the Item	Competitive_Venues	Number
4) Brands Competing with the Item	Similar_Brands	Number
5) Physical Performance	Performance	{10..0}
6) Packaging	Packaging	{10..0}
7) Vendor Reputation	Reputation	{10..0}
8) Expected Category Performance	Category_Potential	{10..0}
9) Total Vendor Support	Vendor_Support	{10..0}

B. Supplied by the Vendor

Description	Abbreviation	Type
1) The Item Under Consideration	Item_Name	String
2) Manufacturer	Vendor_Name	String
3) Buyer Presented with the Item	Buyer_Name	String
4) Suggested Retail Price	Retail_Price	Dollars
5) Unit Cost	Wholesale_Price	Dollars
6) Items per Case	Case_Lot_Size	Number
7) Cases per Cubic Foot	Cases_Per_Cube	Number
8) Weight of a Case	Case_Weight	Pounds
9) Cost of a Delivered Case	Buyer_Case_Cost	Dollars
10) Minimum Case Order	Minimum_Order	Number
11) Lead Time	Lead_Time	Days
12) Shipping Company	Shipper	String
13) Shipping Method	Shipped_By	String
14) Shelf Life	Shelf_Life	Days
15) Stock Protection	Replacement	Yes/No
16) Sale Guarantee	Guarantee	Yes/No
17) How Long on Market	Duration	Years

C. Decisions

Accept/Reject
Continue/Withdraw

---

time-consuming. Management's commitment is essential for successful development, testing, and evaluation. We visualize the use of such expert systems in various retail organizations for the decision problems of retail buyers in the near future. Although the model, as we have conceptualized it, applies only to new product acceptance or rejection, it is logical to expect this model to be integrated into or extended into other parts of a retailer's information system. Such expert systems can be envisioned in category reviews with vendors, product performance

Figure 6.2
Examples of Special Data Tables

A. The Table Name Is: INTERACTIVE-BUYERS-VENDORS

Interactive
    Buyers
        Vendors
            => Marketing Strategy
            => WholesaleTransaction

            Marketing Strategy:
                (The_Item,   is-marketed-by)
                (Vendor_Name,   markets)

                Column Headings from Production are:
                    The_Item, Vendor_Name

            WholesaleTransaction:
                (The_Item,   is sold by)
                (Vendor_Name,   sells)

                Column Headings from WholesaleTransaction are:
                    The_Item, Vendor_Name

            Column Headings for Table Interactive-Buyers-Vendors are:
            The_Item, Vendor_Name

B. This Table Name Is: VALUE-NONECONOMIC-SUBJECTIVE-RELATIONS

Role	Entity_1	Relation	Entity_2
Physical Performance	The_Item	performs	Performance
Physical Performance	Performance	is-the-performance-of	The_Item
Product Packaging	The_Item	is-packed	Packaging
Product Packaging	Packaging	is-the-packaging-of	The_Item
Vendor Reputation	Reputation	is-the-reputation-of	The_Item

168

Figure 6.3
Illustration of Logistic Regression in the Knowledge Base

Logistic.Regression.Input

Acceptance	Performance	Packaging	Reputation

This table can be constructed by the following SQL statements.

```
CREATE TABLE Logistic.Regression.Input
(Acceptance    SMALLINT    NOT NULL,
 Performance   SMALLINT    NOT NULL,
 Packaging     SMALLINT    NOT NULL,
 Reputation    SMALLINT    NOT NULL)

INSERT INTO Logistic.Regression.Input
          (Performance, Packaging, Reputation)
SELECT Performance, Packaging, Reputation
FROM  Value-NonEconomic-Subjective
```

Now the Acceptance column needs defined binary values.

```
INSERT INTO Logistic.Regression.Input
          (Acceptance)
SELECT      The_Decision
FROM        Decision-Table
```

The Logistic.Regression.Input is submitted to a statistical calculation procedure. That procedure returns the coefficients, standard error, and statistical significance of each coefficient. There is one coefficient for each column of Logistic.Regression.Input except the first column (the dependent variable).

The information is returned in a table that is created and specified when the procedure is given the input. This output table, in this case, appears thus:

Logistic.Regression.Output

Variable	Coefficient	Standard Error	Statistical Significance
Performance	X_1	Y_1	Z_1
Packaging	X_2	Y_2	Z_2
Reputation	X_3	Y_3	Z_3

reviews, the identification of candidates to discontinue, as well as service-level reviews. Inventory management, in both the store and warehouse, is another area ideally suited to the development of such an expert system. In fact, the quantitative rules and logic of the typical inventory and shelf management areas make them perfect choices for extensions of the expert system model put forth here.

7

SUMMARY

The preceding chapters have covered issues and methods related to a trade buyer's acceptance of a new product presented to the supermarket organization for resale. In addition to presenting the results of a comprehensive empirical analysis based on a large number of actual new products and hypothetical new products, we have shown how the models can be utilized to the advantage of both manufacturers and supermarket chain organizations. Against this background, we will discuss some limitations, potential remedies, and implications of our research and future directions.

LIMITATIONS AND POTENTIAL REMEDIES

Our data collection efforts were somewhat disappointing because key pieces of information were missing (e.g., exact number of coupons, dollar amounts of advertising) for several actual new products. This is not simply a researcher's problem; the problem of missing information is a concern for retailer buyers as well. We believe that information from vendors could be much improved by the inclusion, perhaps even standardization, of advertising and promotional materials, discounting schedules, and other information in new product packets. Although some vendors may consider such a proposal as threatening because of feared loss of competitive advantage (loss, for example, of their own unique format of presentation), the overall effect of standardization would undoubtedly increase the efficiency of the entire marketing system for grocery products.

Our attempts to supplement the analysis of decisions on actual new products by data from hypothetical new products have been somewhat incomplete because of the difficulty of the data collection tasks. Although we have provided realistic scenarios of hypothetical new products, each described on a number of relevant attributes, it appears to us that the buyers found the subsequent judgmental task quite difficult. In this respect, our goal of comprehensive analysis has been only partially fulfilled. Further work could refine this effort on collecting data on hypothetical new products and combine the results with those of actual decisions. Also, hypothetical new products data collection could serve the purposes of tracking new buyers in a retail organization.

Although the channel intermediary selected for this study, a corporate wholesale-retail chain, is deemed to be representative in the grocery industry, we stress that the generalizability of the results may be limited. Thus, this line of research should be extended to determine the degree of interfirm (intermediary) differences among additional channel intermediaries in the grocery industry. It is likely that the different strategies and different organizational structures of voluntary and cooperative wholesalers, convenience store companies, and other nontraditional supermarket formats would make a substantial difference in the standard operating procedure of buyers, a different set of decision rules for acceptance, and thus a likely different set of managerial and policy recommendations.

The research methods implemented here could be easily extended to other industries such as books, movie theaters, records, videos, and computer software – all businesses where decisions on selection need to be made from a universe composed of a far greater number of products than can possibly be accommodated by the intermediary firm (often a wholesale or retail outlet). Examination of the new product additions and deletions process in these industries has not been undertaken. Such a research effort would assist us in understanding the decision processes of the intermediaries in general.

MANAGERIAL IMPLICATIONS

The results of the modeling of the accept-reject decisions for new items by one channel intermediary are significant, and the explanatory variables generally behave as predicted. Such results, especially when refined and validated with subsequent analyses, should prove useful to both firm managers and public policy makers.

Our analysis approach should prove useful to manufacturers in the new product development process, especially in marketing budget allocation decisions. The diagnostic statistics for our models are highly significant. In particular, grocery product marketers are regularly forced to make resource allocation decisions with little information about the probabilities of likely outcomes. Operating under limited budgets, a marketing manager of a packaged goods firm might need information about the expected payoff from additional investment in marketing effort, say couponing or television advertising, for a proposed new product or from extending the line or family of a current product or category. Our analysis suggests that the appropriate response to such a question depends, among others, on the product's price and its product category. Specifically, there is a positive nonsignificant impact on buyer acceptance when a low-priced item (under $1.00) is evaluated as part of a family; the opposite result seems to hold when the item is priced over $1.00 (medium price), and a significant negative effect is seen for items over $2.00 (high price).

Another example is the effectiveness of marketing research. The results of our study show clearly that both test marketing and marketing research favorably dispose buyers to accept new products. Buyers interviewed on this question reported that although they recognize the possibility that any research presented by a manufacturer may be biased somewhat in favor of that manufacturer's product, they are able to adjust for this expected bias and evaluate the research results accordingly. However, market research and test marketing costs have escalated dramatically in recent years. Marketing managers clearly have to weigh the costs of such research with the value of the higher probability of acceptance that such research is likely to produce.

Although new product introductions have been widely cited as one of the major modes of conduct of grocery manufacturers, new products are likely to be an equally important strategic tool of distributors as well. Indeed, many retailers are beginning to handle and merchandise new products in special ways: new product space in the weekly advertisement, dedicated space in the store for new products, and in-store demonstration of new products to generate consumer interest, among others. Yet little research has probed the conduct of the retail buying teams, gatekeepers to the supermarket shelves, regarding how they decide to accept or reject the growing number of new product offerings. The statistical model developed in this book estimated the importance of the various components of a manufacturer's new product strategy in determining the acceptance of a new product by an individual supermarket intermediary. With knowledge of manufacturer new product budgets, these results can be used in the calculation of marginal returns associated with various marketing mix factors and optimum levels and allocation of manufacturer expenditures. When the optimal decisions are implemented, systemwide efficiency increases; profits can be higher for channel members, and prices can be lower for consumers.

SYSTEMWIDE IMPLICATIONS

The lack of significant positive effects of certain terms of trade (e.g., slotting allowance and free cases) and, indeed, the significant negative effect of others (e.g., bill-back provisions) have several implications for total food system efficiency. Although this result appears contrary to certain of the conduct model's prior expectations and contrary to much popular industry perception, a possible hypothesis is that the presence of certain nonprice incentives, like slotting allowances, may be correlated with inferior products. That is, suppliers may offer additional support for products they fear are not truly unique, and buyers may recognize and accept truly superior products on their own merits without requiring additional inducements. In fact, when the buyers in the participating retail firm were confronted with this initially puzzling result, they corroborated that the hypothesis accurately described typical industry practice. Moreover, the attribute profile of products that had withstood the test of the marketplace – those selling well after two years – suggests that buyers apparently "overestimated" the importance of the slotting allowances (the index was 1.38). This finding also suggests that buyers may initially accept products that are accompanied by slotting allowances, perhaps because of the financial incentive alone, only to discontinue them relatively sooner than competing new items without slotting allowances.

The implication is that much of the large and currently expanding manufacturer promotional allowances directed to the retail trade may be inefficient, if not redundant. Manufacturers may be better off by reallocating some of their new product budgets into activities more likely to influence both buyers and consumers positively. However, this is not an easy prescription because, as this analysis has shown, several of the strategy variables that are most influential with buyers (e.g., product uniqueness and category growth) are apparently not weighted as heavily by consumers. That is, retail buyers base new product decisions, at least in part, on a different set of criteria from consumers. Better prediction by retail buyers of ultimate product preference by their consumers is likely to increase both firm and system efficiency.

Subsequent to the first round of research findings, extensive discussions were held with the buyers to gain further insights into various industry interpretations of the results. The buyers, in general, were not surprised by what we found. In many instances, they explained that problems existed, or at least performance was less than optimal, because of breakdowns in communication between buyer and seller. The low rating given by the buyers to the quality of the vendor presentation and the significant negative impact of bill-back provisions are evidence that vendors could improve their own, and probably systemwide, performance by listening more effectively to what the buyers say they want and need. Although manufacturers were not interviewed on this same score, it is undoubtedly equally true that retailers, too, could profit and improve system performance by better communication to sellers as well. Exhibit 7.1 provides several industry perspectives on this important issue. Better buyer-seller coordination, pointed to in our studies, will result in improved grocery system performance.

Exhibit 7.1
How Can Suppliers Become More Knowledgeable about the Specific Needs and Preferences of Their Various Retail Customers?

At a recent roundtable discussion sponsored by the grocery industry trade weekly, *Supermarket News,* retailers, wholesalers, and manufacturers shared their ideas on a number of topics. One of the key points stressed was the need for clear open lines of communication among the different segments of the industry.

How can the suppliers become more knowledgeable about retail customers' needs and goals? Robert Ingram, vice-president of merchandising for Roger Williams Foods Incorporated, suggests spending more time with the salesperson. In the New England area, he points out, "sometimes new sales people get five days with the existing salesman, and have to cover twenty or thirty accounts, both at the retail and warehouse level." Thomas Lowe, vice-president of merchandising for Price Chopper Supermarkets, feels that it is the responsibility of the manufacturer to know the marketplace, while the retailers have the task of communicating their special needs as a company.

With all the movement in the industry, especially within various accounts, when buyers are moved from category to category, some merchandisers express concern that educating personnel is almost a hopeless task. Paul Reuter of *Supermarket Insights,* a firm that produces grocery industry video magazines, points out, "Today, the retailer has more responsibility to let the manufacturing community know what they are all about. I think you've got to rethink your position to a particular philosophy rather than rely on appointment days and buying hours, and go on to the next step."

But what is that next step? Manufacturers feel that the retailers should put out a guidebook for the industry on what *they* expect from store calls. The retailers should be able to communicate about their personnel "who they are, what they are responsible for, and so on, so that manufacturers know who to contact to get things done," says Brooke Lennon, vice-president of merchandising for Grand Union Company.

Manufacturers and retailers agree that the most important element of the process is the sales rep. Proper communication between the different segments should equip the rep to face calls with a maximum of knowledge and a minimum of confusion. Once again, it is the networking among the industry's basic components that paves the way for the efficient marketing of any product.

All participants in the discussion agreed that new product introduction is an extremely valuable component of the industry, but many complained that the introduction process is flawed. In order to keep lines of communication among manufacturers, wholesalers, and retailers open, the panel came up with some suggestions.

Exhibit 7.1 (*cont.*)

Retailers request that the manufacturers' reps who are pitching the product be well informed about the retailer or wholesaler they are approaching. Dialogue at all stages is essential so that the manufacturer and retailer can work together to launch the product successfully. The retailers also suggest that the manufacturer offer the introductory allowance for a reasonable period after the coupon drops – at least two to four weeks.

Manufacturers ask that retailers speed up the decision-making process after new product presentations. If a retailer rejects the product, the manufacturers also request an explanation. A retailer who decides to buy into the new product should do so early so that the manufacturers can move up advertising schedules and extend introductory deals beyond the coupon drop date.

Both sides agree that communication is essential. Dialogues between retailers and manufacturers keep both sides aware of special needs, making the process of new product development easier for all parties.

Finally, our data show that a higher percentage of products were accepted when market research results were presented (39 percent of products with test marketing or marketing research results were accepted versus 28 percent acceptance rate for products without these results). As a result, one could suggest that, given the high costs of test marketing a new item with consumers, manufacturers instead simply introduce the item. Buyers frequently are in a better position than a manufacturer to assess potential consumer demand. Thus, this procedure may serve as a quick and inexpensive market test. In this sense, recent large numbers of new product introductions may not represent inefficient product proliferation but an efficient manufacturer strategy to increase variety (and profit) while reducing systemwide costs.

FUTURE RESEARCH DIRECTIONS

Based on this research experience with one company, we are encouraged that a richer complement of conduct or strategic variables can be incorporated into economic analysis to improve managerial effectiveness, systemwide efficiency, and performance. Further investigation is warranted into the idea that emerged in this research that buyers and consumers may use different sets of variables in evaluating new products.

While the empirical approach we used has enabled us to describe the judgmental processes of a retail buyer, arguments can be made that we still seek a solid theoretical foundation for the estimated model. The development of a model based on microeconomic theory in which an intermediary's decision to add a new product is one of maximizing the utility of the retail firm could be a worthwhile pursuit. Such a model may include such theoretical constructs as product quality, organizational innovativeness, and competitive advantage, which can lead directly to specification of variables to be included in an analytical model for estimation.

Another obvious direction of future research is to replicate this research with additional firms to probe such questions as: Why do certain firms choose particular organizational forms to evaluate new products? What is the impact of these other forms (e.g., no committee) on the acceptance rates? Are some forms more (less) efficient or more (less) beneficial for producers or consumers? Which organizational forms enhance the success of manufacturer strategies? It might be shown, for example, that a reorganization of a distributor's buying process could result in lowering a firm's transaction costs and a probable improvement in system welfare.

A starting point for such research can be found in Exhibit 7.2, which contains an example of a written questionnaire that might be used with a wide sample of grocery industry buyers to elicit the various organization forms, standard decision rules for new product buying, the importance of various criteria in the buying process and the characteristics of the intermediary firm itself, and how these criteria relate to and influence the acceptance and deletion decisions for the firm's product portfolio.

An ideal next step in this research stream is to develop a societal balance sheet of costs and benefits coming from the new product introduction activity in the food system. This has been attempted before, but the results have always been inconclusive. However, with the type of data available in this study, it should be possible to improve on the estimates and conclusions of former studies. Various measurement questions arise in this endeavor. From the manufacturer's perspective, not only are assessments of costs of R&D and marketing effort needed, but so are the opportunity costs of false introductions and early dismissal of likely successes. Further, the importance of new products for the viability of the firms should be measured in monetary terms. Similar costs and benefits can be identified at the intermediary level. While one can debate the existence of any consumer benefits at all from new product proliferation, ample research opportunities are available to increase the efficiency of the process.

It would be useful to investigate the potential interactive effects among the variables included in the model. This work could explore the differential effects of various product groups on buyer decisions. Our

Exhibit 7.2
An Illustrative Survey of Trade Buyer Practices in the New Item Evaluation Process

---

1. About how many new item presentations do you listen to in an average week?

5 or less	_____
6 to 10	_____
11 to 15	_____
16 to 20	_____
21 or more	_____

2. On average, how much time do you spend, after each new item presentation, evaluating each new item? _____ minutes

3. On average, how would you grade the information presented?

A	_____
B	_____
C	_____
D	_____
F	_____

4. Out of every 10 new items offered, how many are accepted? _____

5. How long is a new item given to prove itself? _____ months

6. In accepting an item, is it your policy to discontinue another item at the same time?

Usually	_____
Sometimes	_____
Never	_____

7. If an item is discontinued, is it usually from the same manufacturer which is introducing the new item?

Yes	_____
No	_____

8. For accepted new items, please indicate who determines, for the retail store, each of the following:

	Headquarters	Stores
Set retail price	_____	_____
Authorize initial distribution	_____	_____
Discontinue item to make room	_____	_____
Use of special display	_____	_____
Determine location in store	_____	_____
Determine shelf position	_____	_____
Determine number of facings	_____	_____
Re-order new items	_____	_____

9. What is your policy regarding manufacturer sales representatives/brokers calls on stores for new items?

They are encouraged	_____
They are discouraged	_____
They are not allowed	_____
We have no policy	_____

10. In deciding to take on a new item, how important do you consider each of the following points that can be made for a new item? (Rate each on a scale of 1 to 100 with 100 being the most important.)

Introductory terms (Ad/display allowances, discounts, how paid, buy-in time) _____

Consumer Advertising (TV, print, spending, frequency) _____

Consumer Promotion (Couponing, premiums, cents off, sampling, etc.) _____

Why item was developed (Consumer need, better product, line extension, etc.) _____

Manufacturer reputation/track record _____

Exhibit 7.2 (*cont.*)

Description of item (Name, contents, size pack) _____

Financial aspects of the item (Cost, margin data) _____

Consumer acceptance (Test market information, product test results) _____

Manufacturer-supplied store merchandising, ideas/materials (Planograms, POP materials) _____

11. How many members sit on the buying committee? _____

12. Does buying committee membership rotate? Yes _____
    No _____

13. How long is the average buying committee meeting? _____ hours

14. How often does the buying committee meet?
More than once each week	_____
Once each week	_____
Once every two weeks	_____
Once every three weeks	_____
Once a month	_____
Less than once a month	_____

15. How many items does your buying committee review per year? _____

16. Of every 10 items received by the buying committee, how many are accepted? _____

17. Can manufacturer sales representatives personally present their new items to the buying committee? Yes _____
    No _____

18. Can a rejected item be reconsidered at another time? Yes _____
    No _____

19. During the past year, how many new items were added to your stores? _____

20. During the past year, how many items were dropped from your stores? _____

21. How many SKU's in total are in your stores? _____

---

work has pointed, for example, to the differential effects that subgroups of our criteria (e.g., high support versus low support and high price versus low price) have on buyer acceptance. Such subgroup analysis is at the heart of what buyers and marketers need to know for the more effective decision making required for specific product strategies. This should be an especially fertile area for research. Next, simultaneous modeling of profit-potential judgments and actual decisions could lead to a better predictive model. Additionally, work is needed to identify reasons for poor prediction by the model. In this context, intensified interaction with decision makers could help considerably in improving the model structure.

Although we focus on the product addition problem, there is a need to formalize the product deletion process as well. Most buying committees apparently engage in the deletion task simultaneously with the addition task. Moreover, examination of sales trends of accepted items should help us determine the new product characteristics that are predictive of long-run marketplace success. Finally, from a public policy viewpoint, it would be of interest to estimate the impact of channel intermediary procurement behavior on producer and consumer welfare.

REFERENCES

Adams, W.J., and J. L. Yellen. (1976). "Commodity Bundling and the Burden of Monopoly." *Quarterly Journal of Economics* 90 (August):475–98.

Advertising Age. (1989). "Leading National Advertisers." (September 27):38.

Bagozzi, Richard P. (1986). *Principles of Marketing Management.* Chicago: Science Research Associates.

Buchanan, B., and E. Shortliffe. (1984). *Rule Based Expert Systems.* Reading, Mass.: Addison-Wesley.

Bucklin, Randolph E., and Diane H. Schmalensee. (1987). *Viewpoints on the Changing Consumer Goods Distribution Scene: Summary of a Marketing Science Institute Conference May 19 and 20, 1987.* Cambridge: Marketing Science Institute.

Burke, Raymond R., Arvind Rangaswamy, Jerry Wind, and Jehoshua Eliashberg. (1988). "ADCAD: A Knowledge-Based System for Advertising Design." Wharton Working Paper 88-027. December.

Buzzell, Robert D., and Robert E. M. Nourse. (1967). *Product Innovation in Food Processing, 1954–1964.* Boston: Division of Research, Harvard Business School.

Buzzell, John A., John A. Quelch, and Walter J. Salmon. (1990). "The Costly Bargain of Trade Promotion." *Harvard Business Review* (March-April, 1990):141–49.

Census of Manufacturers. (1982). *Enterprise Statistics,* U.S. Department of Commerce, Bureau of the Census.

Chevalier, Michel, and Ronald C. Curhan. (1976). "Retail Promotions as a Function of Trade Promotions: A Descriptive Analysis." *Sloan Management Review* 18 (Fall):19–32.

Connor, John M. (1981). "Food Product Proliferation: A Market Structure Analysis." *American Journal of Agricultural Economics* 63 (November):607–17.

Connor, John M., Richard T. Rogers, Bruce W. Marion, and Willard F. Mueller. (1985). *The Food Manufacturing Industries: Structure, Strategies, Performance, and Policies.* Lexington, Mass.: D. C. Heath.

Cooper, R. G. (1980). "Project New Prod: Factors in New Product Success."
  European Journal of Marketing 14(2):227–92.
———. (1982). "New Product Success in Industrial Firms." *Industrial Market-
  ing Management* 11(3):215–23.
Cornell University. (1989). "Operating Results of Food Chains, 1987–88." Re-
  search Report.
Crawford, C. Merle. (1979). "New Product Failure Rates – Facts and Fallacies."
  International Journal of Research Management Vol. 22 No. 5 (Septem-
  ber):9.
Curhan, Ronald C., and Robert J. Kopp. (1986). "Factors Influencing Grocery
  Retailers' Support of Trade Promotions." Marketing Science Institute
  Working Paper 86-104.
———. (1987–88). "Obtaining Retailer Support for Trade Deals: Key Success
  Factors." *Journal of Advertising Research* 27 (December 1987–January
  1988):51–60.
Davis, R., and D. Lenat. (1980). *Knowledge-Base Systems in Artificial Intelli-
  gence.* New York: McGraw-Hill.
Deloitte & Touche. (1990). "Managing the Process of Introducing and Deleting
  Products in the Grocery and Drug Industries." (June).
DFS-Dorland. (1986). *New Product News.* Chicago: Gorman Publishing.
Dixit, A. K., and J. E. Stiglitz. (1977). "Monopolistic Competition and Optimal
  Product Diversity." *American Economic Review* 67 (June):297–308.
Doyle, Peter, and Charles Weinberg. (1973). "Effective New Product Decisions
  for Supermarkets." *Operational Research Quarterly* 24 (March):45–54.
Federal Trade Commission. (1990). "Economic Issues: A Review of Structure –
  Performance Studies in Grocery Retailing." Washington D.C.: Bureau of
  Economics.
Food Marketing Institute. (1986, 1989, 1990). "The State of the Food Market-
  ing Industry Speaks." Washington, D.C.: FMI.
Fortune. (1986). "The King of Suds Reigns Again." August.
Friedman, Martin, ed. (1990). *Gorman's New Product News.*
Gallagher, John P. (1988). *Knowledge Systems for Business: Integrating Ex-
  pert Systems and MIS.* Englewood Cliffs, N.J.: Prentice-Hall.
Gallo, Anthony E. (1990). "The Food Marketing System in 1989." *Agricultural
  Information Bulletin,* no. 603 (May). Washington, D.C.: USDA.
Gorman Publishing Co. (1990). *Prepared Foods: New Products Annual.* Vol.
  159, no. 8.
Grashof, John F. (1970). "Supermarket Chain Product Mix Decision Criteria: A
  Simulation   Experiment."   *Journal   of   Marketing   Research*   7
  (May):235–42.
Grunert, K. G. (1984). "Consumer Information Systems in Videotex: Design
  and Acceptance." *Journal of Consumer Studies and Home Economics*
  8:183–98.
Hamm, Larry G. (1981a). "Food Distributor Procurement Practices: Their Im-
  plications for Food System Structure and Coordination." Ph.D. disserta-
  tion, Michigan State University.
———. (1981b). "The Impact of Food Distributor Procurement Practices on
  Food System Structure and Coordination." N.C. Project 117, WP-58,
  University of Wisconsin.

Hardy, Kenneth G. (1986). "Key Success Factors for Manufacturers' Sales Promotions in Package Goods." *Journal of Marketing* 50(July):13–23.

Harman, Paul, and David King. (1985). *Expert Systems.* New York: John Wiley.

Harrell, Frank E. (1985). "The LOGIST Procedure." In *SAS User's Guide.* Cary, N.C.: SAS Institute.

Hayes-Roth, Frederick, Donald A. Waterman, and Douglas B. Lenat. (1983). *Building Expert Systems.* Reading, Mass.: Addison-Wesley.

Heeler, Roger M., Michael J. Kearney, and Bruce J. Mehaffey. (1973). "Modeling Supermarket Product Selection." *Journal of Marketing Research* 10(February):34–37.

Henderson, D. R. (1975). "Toward a Theory of Vertical Market Behavior." NC-117 Working Paper. 2 October.

Hisrich, Robert D., and Michael P. Peters. (1984). *Marketing Decisions for New Mature Products: Planning Development and Control.* Columbus: C. E. Merrill.

Holsapple, Clyde W., and Andrew B. Whinston. (1987). *Business Expert Systems.* New York: Irwin.

Horowitz, Abraham D., and J. Edward Russo. (1989). "Modeling New Car Consumer-Salesperson Interaction for a Knowledge-Based System." In Thomas K. Srull, (ed.), *Advances in Consumer Research,* vol. 16. Ann Arbor: Association for Consumer Research.

Kotler, Philip. (1988). *Marketing Management: Analysis, Planning, Implementation, and Control.* Englewood Cliffs, N.J.: Prentice-Hall.

Kuczmarski, T. D. (1988). *Managing New Products.* Englewood Cliffs, N.J.: Prentice-Hall.

Kumara, S., A. Soyster, and R. L. Kashyap. (1986). "Artificial Intelligence Series, Part 1: An Introduction to Artificial Intelligence." *Industrial Engineering* (December):8–20.

Lancaster, Kelvin J. (1975). "Socially Optimal Product Differentiation." *American Economic Review* 62:567–85.

Leed, Theodore W. and Gene A. German. (1985). *Food Merchandising: Principles and Practices.* New York: Lebhar-Friedman.

Leibenstein, H. (1979). "A Branch of Economics Is Missing: Micro-Micro Theory." *Journal of Economic Literature* 17:477–502.

Levy, Michael, John Webster, and Roger Kerin. (1983). "Formulating Push Marketing Strategies: A Method and Application." *Journal of Marketing* 47 (Winter):25–34.

Liebowitz, Jay. (1990). *The Dynamics of Decision Support Systems and Expert Systems.* Chicago: Dryden Press.

McCann, John M. (1986). *The Marketing Workbench: Using Computers for Better Performance.* New York: Dow Jones-Irwin.

McLaughlin, Edward W., and Vithala R. Rao. (1988). "An Exploratory Modeling of the Decision Process for New Product Selection by Supermarket Buyers." *Agribusiness: An International Journal* 4 (April):177–85.

Maidique M. A., and B. J. Zirger. (1984). "A Study of Success and Failure in Product Innovation: The Case of the U.S. Electronics Industry." *IEEE Transactions on Engineering Management,* EM-31(4):192–203. November.

Marion, B. W. (1976). "Application of the Structure, Conduct, Performance Paradigm to Subsector Analysis." NC-117 Working Paper 7. November.
———. (1986). *The Organization and Performance of the U.S. Food System.* Lexington, Mass.: Lexington Books.
Marketing News. (1987). "Mergers, Acquisitions in Food Industry Set Record in 1986." June 5.
Martins, G. (1984). "The Overselling of Expert Systems." *Datamation,* November 1.
Montgomery, David B. (1973). "New Product Distribution: An Analysis of Supermarket Buyer Decisions." *Journal of Marketing Research* 12 (August):255-64.
Morrison, Donald G. (1969). "On the Interpretation of Discriminant Analysis." *Journal of Marketing Research* 6 (May):156-63.
New York Times. (1988). "For New Products, Entry Free Is High." January 7.
Nielsen, A. C. (1987). *Nielsen Early Intelligence Systems.* Chicago: Nielsen.
Nilson, N. J. (1980). *Principles of Artificial Intelligence.* Palo Alto: Tioga Press.
———. (1971). *Problem Solving Methods in Artificial Intelligence.* New York: McGraw-Hill.
O'Neal, Kim R. (1987). "Artificial Intelligence Part 3: Round-table Participants Discuss Artificial Intelligence." *Industrial Engineering* (February): 52-63.
Padberg, Daniel I., and Randall E. Westgren. (1979). "Product Competition and Consumer Behavior in the Food Industries." *American Journal of Agricultural Economics* 61:620-25.
Parks, Michael W. (1987). "Artificial Intelligence Part 2: Expert Systems Fill in the Missing Link." *Industrial Engineering* (January):36-45.
Pau, L. F., J. Motivala, Y. H. Pao, and H. H. Teh. (eds.) (1989). *Expert Systems in Economics, Banking and Management.* Amsterdam: North-Holland.
Pessemier, Edgar A. (1982). *Product Management: Strategy and Organization.* New York: Wiley.
Pratt, Philip J. (1990). *A Guide to SQL.* Boston: Boyd & Fraser.
Progressive Grocer. (1987). "New Items: Behind the Hits and Misses." Executive Rep. Series. October.
———. (1987). "New Item Special Report." (December).
———. (1989). *Annual Report of Grocery Industry – 1989.* (April).
———. (1990). *Annual Report of the Grocery Industry – 1990.* (April).
Rao, Vithala R., and Edward W. McLaughlin. (1989). "Modeling the Decision to Add New Products by Channel Intermediaries." *Journal of Marketing* 53:80-88.
Robinson, Patrick J. (1981). "Comparison of Pre-Test Market New-Product Forecasting Models." In *New-Product Forecasting,* 181-204. Edited by Y. Wind, V. Mahajan, and R. N. Cardozo. Lexington, Mass.: Lexington Books.
Rogers, R. T., and J. A. Caswell. (1988). "Strategic Management and the Internal Organization of Food Marketing Firms." *Agribus* 4:3-10.
Rothwell, R. (1972). *Factors for Success in Industrial Innovations: Project SAPPHO – A Comparative Study of Success and Failure in Industrial Innovation.* Science Policy Research Unit, University of Sussex, Brighton, U.K.

Russo, J. Edward. (1987). "Toward Intelligent Product Information Systems." *Journal of Consumer Policy* 10:109–38.

Salomon Brothers. (1988). "The Corporate Financial Statements of the SSP 400 and Selected Industry Groups." New York: Salomon Brothers, Inc.

Scherer, F. M. (1980). *Industrial Market Structure and Economic Performance.* 2d ed. Chicago: Rand-McNally Company.

———. (1979). "The Welfare Economics of Product Variety: An Application to the Ready-to-Eat Cereals Industry." *Journal of Industrial Economics* 28 (December):113–34.

Schmalensee, Richard. (1978). "Entry Deterrence in the Ready-to-Eat Breakfast Cereal Industry." *Bell Journal of Economics* 9 (Autumn):305–27.

Shaffer, J. D. (1980). "Food System Organization and Performance: Toward a Conceptual Framework." *American Journal of Agricultural Economics* 62:310–18.

Spence, A. M. (1976). "Product Differentiation and Welfare." *American Economic Review* 66:707–14.

Sprague, Jr., Ralph H., and Hugh J. Watson. (eds.) (1989). *Decision Support Systems: Putting Theory into Practice.* 2d ed. Englewood Cliffs, N.J.: Prentice-Hall.

Stern, Louis W. (1987). "The Changing Power Structure and Channel Strategy." In *Viewpoints on the Changing Consumer Goods Distribution Scene: Summary of a Marketing Science Institute Conference.* Edited by R. E. Bucklin and D. H. Schmalensee. Cambridge, Mass.: Marketing Science Institute.

Stern, Nicholas. (1972). "The Optimal Size of Market Areas." *Journal of Economic Theory* 4:154–73.

Supermarket News. (1984a). "Distributor Demand Sharpens for New Product Incentives." August 27.

Supermarket News. (1984b). "Dialog, New Products and Their Implications." December 17.

Turban, Efraim. (1988). *Decision Support and Expert Systems, Managerial Perspectives.* New York: Macmillan.

Urban, Glen L. and John R. Hauser. (1980). *Design and Marketing of New Products.* Englewood Cliffs, N.J.: Prentice-Hall.

USDA. (1990). "Food Marketing Review. 1989–90." Economic Research Service, *Agricultural Economic Report,* Number 639.

van der Lans, Rick F. (1988). *Introduction to SQL.* Translated by Andrea Gray. Reading, Mass.: Addison-Wesley.

Vloyanetes, P., and M. Magel. (1986). "Electronic Retailing." *Marketing Communications* 2 (May):31–34, 37, 79.

Walker, Strother H., and David B. Duncan. (1967). "Estimation of the Probability of an Event as a Function of Several Independent Variables." *Biometrika* 54:167–78.

Walker, Teri C., and Richard K. Miller. (1990). *Expert Systems Handbook: An Assessment of Technology and Applications.* Liburn, Ga.: Fairmont Press.

Westgren, R. E., and M. L. Cook. (1986). "Strategic Management and Planning." *Research Issues in Agribusiness Management,* Proceedings of Post-Conference Workshop, AAEA annual meeting, Reno, July 30–31.

Williamson, M. (1985). *Artificial Intelligence for Microcomputers*. New York: Bradley/Simon and Schuster.

Wind, Yoram. (1982). *Product Policy: Concepts, Methods and Strategy*. Reading, Mass.: Addison-Wesley.

Wittink, Dick R., and Philippe Cattin. (1989). "Commercial Use of Conjoint Analysis: An Update." *Journal of Marketing* 53 (July):91–96.

Zellner, James A. (1989). "A Simultaneous Analysis of Food Industry Conduct." *American Journal of Agricultural Economics* 71:105–15.

INDEX

About the Authors

EDWARD W. McLAUGHLIN is Assistant Professor of Distribution
and Marketing in the Department of Agricultural Economics at Cornell University. His research has encompassed a wide variety of marketing topics in the food industry, and he regularly leads workshops
and seminars for food companies.

VITHALA R. RAO is Professor of Marketing and Quantitative Methods in the Johnson Graduate School of Management at Cornell University. His numerous articles have appeared in such journals as
*Marketing Science, Journal of Marketing Research, Journal of Con-
sumer Research,* and *Management Science.*